PENGUIN ⬤ CLASSICS

BAUDELAIRE: SELECTED POEMS

CHARLES-PIERRE BAUDELAIRE was born in Paris in 1821, the only son of an elderly father and young mother. His father died before he was six and his mother remarried a year later. Baudelaire was later to express violent hostility towards his stepfather, Colonel (subsequently General) Aupick.

Wayward at school, he came second in the national Latin verse competition in 1837, but was still expelled from Lycée Louis-le-Grand in 1839. A nominal law student, he fell into bohemian company and his alarmed parents sent him on a long sea voyage to the Indian Ocean. He returned prematurely and was never to travel far from Paris again until his ill-fated journey to Belgium at the end of his life. On his majority in 1842 he moved to a flat on the Ile St-Louis and indulged his artistic tastes so extravagantly that his parents, trying to safeguard what was left of his capital, transferred control of it to the lawyer Ancelle, a well-meaning soul on whom Baudelaire would always vent his resentment at this humiliating situation.

Baudelaire was never again to be free from debt, or from schemes to restore his fortune by writing, publishing or lecturing. He suffered a stroke in Belgium in 1866, lingered on semi-paralysed and, latterly, mute and was brought back to Paris, where he died the following year. His collection of verse, *Les Fleurs du Mal* (1857) was the subject of a prosecution for indecency; six poems were removed from it and not reinstated in France until 1942. Further editions, with more poems, appeared in 1861 and 1868. His prose poems and writings on art and literature were collected after his death; the literary criticism shows the influence of Edgar Allan Poe, whose short stories he also translated.

Baudelaire is known to have had attachments to three women, the longest-lasting to the creole Jeanne Duval. So far as we know he died childless.

Carol Clark is Fellow and Tutor in French at Balliol College, Oxford.

CHARLES BAUDELAIRE

Selected Poems

With a Plain Prose Translation, Introduction and Notes by
CAROL CLARK

PENGUIN BOOKS

PENGUIN BOOKS

Published by the Penguin Group
Penguin Books Ltd, 80 Strand, London WC2R 0RL, England
Penguin Putnam Inc., 375 Hudson Street, New York, New York 10014, USA
Penguin Books Australia Ltd, 250 Camberwell Road, Camberwell, Victoria 3124, Australia
Penguin Books Canada Ltd, 10 Alcorn Avenue, Toronto, Ontario, Canada M4V 3B2
Penguin Books India (P) Ltd, 11 Community Centre, Panchsheel Park, New Delhi – 110 017, India
Penguin Books (NZ) Ltd, Cnr Rosedale and Airborne Roads, Albany, Auckland, New Zealand
Penguin Books (South Africa) (Pty) Ltd, 24 Sturdee Avenue, Rosebank 2196, South Africa

Penguin Books Ltd, Registered Offices: 80 Strand, London WC2R 0RL, England

www.penguin.com

This selection first published 1995
Reprinted with a new Chronology 2004
8

Translation, introduction and notes copyright © Carol Clark, 1995
Chronology copyright © Carol Clark, 2004
All rights reserved

The moral right of the editor has been asserted

Set in 10.5/13 pt Monotype Bembo
Typeset by Datix International Limited, Bungay, Suffolk
Printed in England by Clays Ltd, St Ives plc

CONTENTS

INTRODUCTION

When the first volume of Baudelaire's complete works was published the year after his death, a copy was sent to Prosper Mérimée, a man of taste, a power in the world of art and scholarship, and a considerable writer himself. He wrote to a friend, 'They've sent me Baudelaire's works, which have infuriated me. Baudelaire was mad! He died in the poorhouse after writing some verses that won praise from Victor Hugo, and which had nothing else to recommend them but their indecency. Now they're calling him an unrecognized genius!'

Victor Hugo's name is mentioned in most of the judgements of Baudelaire made soon after his death, and this is to be expected, for Hugo was then, and for long afterwards, regarded as France's greatest poet of the nineteenth century. He was a man of boundless physical and poetic energy: in his eighty-three years of life he published poems, plays, novels and political writings, which in the standard collected edition fill thirty quarto volumes. He also played a significant part in the political upheavals of the century, in turn as an ultra-Royalist, a supporter of constitutional monarchy and a Republican; he was created a *pair de France* in 1845 and, on his return to Paris in 1870, elected to the Assemblée Nationale. On his death he was voted a national funeral; after lying in state under the Arc de Triomphe his body, at his own wish, was borne across Paris in a pauper's hearse amid grieving crowds estimated at two million, before being laid to rest among France's greatest citizens in the Panthéon.

Baudelaire's life and death could hardly have been more different. Apart from a handful of juvenilia and late pieces,

his whole output of verse is contained in one volume, *Les Fleurs du Mal*, which, though it gained a certain notoriety in his lifetime and was admired by the most advanced writers of the day, had little public success. (He was known to the wider public, if at all, as the translator of Poe's tales.) He also wrote a slim volume of prose poems, a long-short story (*La Fanfarlo*), a set of essays on the effects of various drugs (*Les Paradis artificiels*), part of which was a free translation of De Quincey, and a body of art, music and literary criticism which was never collected in his lifetime but now appears as the *Curiosités esthétiques* and *L'Art romantique*. His attempts to win fame and fortune by his writings were always perfectly unsuccessful; his candidature for the French Academy was regarded as absurd, and in 1865 he estimated that twenty-odd years of writing and publishing had brought him little more than fifteen thousand francs – about £600 in the money of the day. Unlike, say, Flaubert, he did not have a reliable private income and spent most of his adult life in the peculiarly painful poverty of the *déclassé*. After a brief flirtation with revolutionary action in 1848 he avoided political involvement of any kind. His health declined sharply from 1864 until his death in 1867, at forty-six (not in the poorhouse but in a private clinic paid for by his friends). He was never mad, in the sense of psychotic, but his behaviour and reasoning were often regarded as strange even by those who loved him, and have given rise to a copious interpretative literature after his death, ranging from the Freudian to the existentialist. For the last year of his life, after several strokes and probably affected by tertiary syphilis, he could not speak, though his friends maintained that his mind was not affected.

He had the final misfortune, for a Parisian, of dying in August, and the most distinguished guests invited to his funeral did not attend. He was hurried to his grave in a summer downpour, attended only by a small group of friends which included Manet and Verlaine. When his fellow poet

Théodore de Banville, speaking his funeral oration, said that in the near future Baudelaire would be recognized as a poet not only of talent but of genius, and that he would haunt the minds of modern men and move them when other artists left them cold, many hearers must have dismissed these words as fanciful, an understandable emotional response to the loss of a beloved friend.

However, Banville's prediction has come true. French readers now have a choice of half a dozen paperback editions of *Les Fleurs du Mal*, and learned libraries contain hundreds of books and probably thousands of articles on his life and writings. Originally condemned for offence against public morals, his poems have found their place on university syllabuses and, final consecration, have recently been set for the *baccalauréat*. The '*poète sinistre, ennemi des familles*' now figures in a series of student guides called 'Les Ecrivains du bac'. But more importantly, his poems are read by many thousands of readers in many countries, not as set texts but for their beauty, their power to move and their continuing modernity. Few now would question Baudelaire's pre-eminence among nineteenth-century poets, indeed among poets generally. While André Gide (b. 1869), asked who was the greatest French poet, still felt obliged to reply '*Victor Hugo, hélas!*', Pierre-Jean Jouve (b. 1887) was firm that

Baudelaire est une origine. Il crée une Poésie française après des siècles de fadeurs et de discours . . .

[Baudelaire is an origin. He creates a French Poetry after centuries of insipidity and holding forth . . .]

Valéry recognized in Baudelaire 'the one modern French poet to be widely read abroad', and by 1930 T. S. Eliot could describe him as 'the greatest exemplar of *modern* poetry in any language', adding that 'his verse and language is the nearest

thing to a complete renovation that we have experienced'.

What, we must wonder, gave Baudelaire's verse this power, after his death, to force a revaluation of what poetry can be and do?

Critical attention paid to Baudelaire in the past has generally focused on the events of his life and their reflection (this process is taken for granted) in his poems. The verse and prose poems are often used as biographical sources in a way a historian might consider dubious. Certainly there is much to tempt the biographer in Baudelaire's life, and still more in what, even in his own day, was called the 'Baudelaire legend', a legend to which the poet himself was at some stages of his life an enthusiastic contributor. Child of an exhausted stock, his father an elderly priest unfrocked under the Revolution, orphaned at six and then wrenched from a life of blissful intimacy by his mother's remarriage to a stern army officer and consoled only by the love of an old nurse; launched on a life of dissipation, and then sent on a long sea voyage to the tropics in the hope of breaking his bad habits and, on return, placed under a strict regime of financial control which meant that he had to beg every penny from the family lawyer; the lover first of a black bit-player, then of a glittering *demi-mondaine*, and finally of a successful but heartless green-eyed actress; haunted by debt, yet a lover of art and collector of pictures and objects which he could not afford, living in sordid lodgings yet always dressed with meticulous care and cleanliness, driven from one expedient to another, writing journalistic pieces against the clock and finally travelling to Belgium, which he loathed, in the quixotic hope of making money by lecturing; seeking escape through drugs and sinking into opium addiction, syphilis, paralysis, aphasia and death. It is easy to see the attraction here for readers of a late Romantic sensibility. Critics of the older school invited the reader's awe at the intensity of the poet's sufferings, while later, more

cynical observers have remarked the extent to which they were self-inflicted or, as Sartre would have it, consciously chosen as a vocation.

This latter view would not in the least have surprised the poet himself, who after all entitled one of his cruellest pieces 'Héautontimorouménos', the self-torturer, and described himself as early as 1844, when he was twenty-two, in these terms:

. . . devant le miroir j'ai perfectionné
L'art cruel qu'un Démon en naissant m'a donné
– De la Douleur pour faire une volupté vraie –
D'ensanglanter son mal et de gratter sa plaie.

[before the mirror I have perfected the cruel art which a Demon endowed me with at my birth, of turning Pain into a real pleasure by making one's wound bleed and scratching one's sore.]

Baudelaire's is studied suffering, studied pleasure and even, perhaps, studied joy, relived in a studied language which was unique at the time of writing and still appears remarkably original today. It is this novel and penetrating poetic language which truly earned him the admiration first of other poets and then of attentive readers until the present day.

One should not pass over in silence the more lurid aspects of Baudelaire's verse, the rather obvious eroticism of some of the pieces and his evident interest in sexual and religious variations like sado-masochism, lesbianism and satanism. Such dangerous delights obviously held an appeal for, say, Swinburne, who was one of the first English writers to express admiration for him, or Aleister Crowley, who translated the prose poems, in fact rather well. But such topics fascinated many artists of the Romantic period (Mario Praz documented them to great effect in *The Romantic Agony*), and the poems they gave rise to are, in general, those which seem to our present taste the

most dated. They are not, therefore, represented heavily in
this selection.

When he leaves behind the over-scented boudoir-cum-
charnel-house, the imagery of Baudelaire's poems is often
consciously modern and consequently unsettling in a less
obvious way. In the 'Tableaux parisiens' he creates a décor of
factory chimneys, omnibuses and dustcarts, and sets one of his
most moving poems amid the debris of Baron Haussmann's
schemes of urban redevelopment. This attempt to make
poetry in and of the modern city was to have been taken
further in the collection of prose poems he was working on at
the time of his fatal stroke, the planned title of which was *Le
Spleen de Paris*. But poetic use of the prosaic is not confined
to these two places. It is frequent, for example, in the love
poetry of 'Spleen et Idéal', where the mistresses invoked are
not semi-divinities but recognizable women who smoke,
dance, sit by charcoal fires, walk with the poet in dark
Parisian streets and, with him, listen to the passage of the
seasons marked not by the song of the nightingale or the
flight of the swallow but by the dull thud on the courtyard
paving-stones of logs being delivered for the winter. These
women wear not vaguely classical drapery but modern
clothes: brightly coloured dresses (77), skirts with flounces
(37), make-up and jewellery (78), and even corsets ('Les
Metamorphoses du Vampire', not translated here). (It is notable
that most of these poems were among those suppressed for
indecency when *Les Fleurs du Mal* was first published; in a
similar way, what gave particular offence about Manet's
Olympia when it was first exhibited in 1865 was not the
figure's nudity but her residual clothing, and the setting
which indicated clearly that she was not a classical goddess or
nymph but a modern high-class prostitute.)

A young poet of the next generation, Laforgue, making
notes in 1885 for an essay on Baudelaire which, sadly, he did
not live long enough to publish, expresses very well the

novelty with which Baudelaire's writing still struck his near contemporaries:

Le premier, [il] parla de Paris en damné quotidien de la capitale (les becs de gaz, les restaurants et leurs soupiraux, les hôpitaux, le jeu, le bois qu'on scie en bûches qui retentissent sur le pavé des cours, et le coin du feu, et les chats, des lits, des bas, des ivrognes et des parfums de fabrication moderne), mais cela de façon noble, lointaine, supérieure.

[He was the first to speak of Paris as one damned to the daily life of the capital (the gas-lamps, the restaurants and their air-vents, the poor-hospitals, gambling, wood being sawn into logs which echo on the paving-stones of the courtyards, and the fireside, and cats, beds, stockings, drunkards and modern, factory-made perfumes), but all in a noble, distant, lofty manner.]

As Laforgue goes on to say, however, it is not only the mention of dustcarts and omnibuses, of stockings and cheap scent, that makes Baudelaire memorably modern. What was even more important was his renewal of the language of poetry; in the notes that survive Laforgue chooses to concentrate on simile and metaphor but also makes some extremely penetrating remarks on vocabulary and metre.

Baudelaire's modernity was all the more striking, and indeed shocking, to his contemporary readers because the conventions of French poetry in his time were so strict. They had, it is true, been loosened to some degree by the previous, Romantic generation of poets, but verse, in both its subject-matter and language, was still supposed to be highly remote from the language and preoccupations of every day. Subjects were to be choice, exalted above the prosaic and if possible morally improving, and language elevated in proportion. Eighteenth-century versifiers and theorists, by refining upon and rendering

even stricter the rules first established in the seventeenth
century, had evolved what was called *le style noble*, of which
eighteenth-century English 'poetic diction' gives some faint
idea. The key concept in both is decorum, or appropriateness.
Certain things (in French a great many) might not be appropri-
ately mentioned in verse at all, unless in the low genre of
burlesque or 'satirical' verse. (In French, this word has connota-
tions of indecency rather than of political incisiveness, because
of the famous seventeenth-century collection of obscene
poems called the *Parnasse satyrique*; Baudelaire's publisher
Poulet-Malassis published a *Nouveau Parnasse satyrique* in Bel-
gium in 1864 which included six poems by Baudelaire, among
them numbers 77 and 78 in this edition.) Unfit for verse were
not only indecent things, but anything down-to-earth, for
example objects in everyday use, or parts of the body apart
from the stylized *main, bras, front* (forehead, but regularly used
as a metonymy for 'face'), *prunelle* (pupil, but used for 'eye'
or 'eyes') or *narine* (nostril, for 'nose': *nez* was taboo). It was
relatively easy, though constricting, to avoid 'low' words in
lyric poetry or on the stage, but the didactic poetry so
popular in the eighteenth century posed serious problems. It
was not easy to write a poem on gardening, like Delille's
'Jardins', when one literally could not call a spade a spade. The
result was that eighteenth-century poets, particularly in the
didactic mode, tied themselves into contortions of circumlocu-
tion to avoid naming the most harmless objects. When Alfred
de Vigny's translation of *Othello* was performed in Paris in
1829, the speaking of the word *mouchoir* (handkerchief) on the
stage caused consternation in the theatre. As late as 1836,
when Alfred de Musset, a man notorious for the freedom of
his own sexual life, wished to refer to prostitutes in a descrip-
tion of the great city in his *Lettre à M. de Lamartine*, he felt
obliged to call them '*de la nuit les prêtresses infâmes*' ('the
infamous priestesses of the night', with a poetic inversion for
good measure). Baudelaire's *catins* (57) would have been un-

thinkable then, and must still have seemed shocking in 1852 when it first appeared. The 'Epilogue' in which Baudelaire sings the praises of Paris, calling her, among other things, an '*énorme catin*' was not published in his lifetime.

It is easy for the modern, English-speaking reader to see how references to whores could shock, but harder for us to realize the impact of the simply prosaic. Baudelaire must surely be the first poet of modern times to lure his mistress away not to a sylvan glade (Alfred de Vigny uncomfortably proposed a caravan!), but to a room with well-polished furniture, coffered ceilings and hothouse flowers (38). In general, his poems make remarkably little reference to what the Romantics meant by Nature; he prefers indoor settings or wholly invented landscapes like those of 60. Invited to contribute to a volume of verses on the theme of Nature, he replied that '*je suis incapable de m'attendrir sur les végétaux*' (I cannot get emotional about the vegetable world), and sent poems 57 and 61, which he said represented his own twilight thoughts.

Conventional poetic style also required decorum in vocabulary. An elevated noun could not be coupled with a homely adjective, or vice versa. Metaphors were to be used sparingly and should not prompt any unedifying thoughts; it was better to confine oneself to those hallowed by time and long use.

Resistance to metaphor in the average reader was so strong that on the appearance of *Les Fleurs du Mal* the reviewer on the *Gazette de Paris* pronounced its title 'not French' and maintained that no one would understand it. Baudelaire deliberately and constantly breaks the rules of decorum and achieves some of his strongest poetic effects through studied mismatches. In an unpublished draft preface to *Les Fleurs du Mal* he said that poetry had the ability

d'exprimer toute sensation de suavité ou d'amertume, de béatitude

ou d'horreur par l'accouplement de tel substantif avec tel adjectif, analogue ou contraire.

[to express any sensation of sweetness or bitterness, of bliss or horror, by the coupling of a given noun with a given adjective, analogous or opposed.]

He attached the greatest importance to metaphor in poetry, writing some forceful pages on the topic in his essay on Victor Hugo (in *L'Art romantique*) and saying of himself:

Je me suis toujours plu à chercher dans la nature extérieure et visible, des exemples et des métaphores qui me servissent à caractériser les jouissances et les impressions d'un ordre spirituel.

[I have always liked to find in outward and visible nature examples and metaphors that would allow me to characterize pleasures and impressions of a spiritual order.]

But the examples he chose (2, 19, 34), and still more the metaphors and comparisons, were often not those that poetic decorum would prescribe.

He is famous for his unexpectedly prosaic comparisons, which use the traditional form of the simile but astonish the reader by the introduction of some everyday object. Laforgue said they '*mettent le pied dans le plat*', put their foot in the dish, a proverbial expression of clumsiness and ill-manners, and described them as 'disconcertingly and invigoratingly tacky'. He singles out '*La nuit s'épaississait ainsi qu'une cloison*' ('night thickened like a wall'). One might add, for instance, '*Quand le ciel bas et lourd pèse comme un couvercle*' (When the low, heavy sky weighs like a lid) or

. . . les vagues terreurs de ces affreuses nuits
Qui compriment le cœur comme un papier qu'on froisse

[the vague terrors of those dreadful nights that grip the heart as one crumples a piece of paper]

or the unlikely metaphor in a poem of praise for his mistress's beauty,

Ta gorge triomphante est une belle armoire
　　　Dont les panneaux bombés et clairs
Comme les boucliers accrochent des éclairs.

[Your triumphant bosom is a fine cupboard whose panels, convex and bright, are like shields catching shafts of light.]

What would have upset conventionally minded readers in these lines is not so much the mention of depression, night terrors or a woman's breasts, but the use of everyday words like *cloison, couvercle, armoire* or *panneau*, particularly in the context of a poetic comparison.

But what of Laforgue's *'façon noble, lointaine, supérieure'*? This phrase seems to point to a tone far removed from deliberate shock tactics. And indeed a kind of seductive remoteness is one of the most distinctive characteristics of Baudelaire's poetic voice.

　　It is partly a question of mode of address. Romantic poetry still, in general, employed the ample periods and declamatory tone of traditional rhetorical discourse. The reader is firmly cast in the role of listener at a performance which (despite the frequent imparting of personal confidences) is essentially public. Baudelaire's poetic voice is usually quieter, more private. As Laforgue went on to say, *'Il se tient bien . . . Jamais il ne se bat les flancs, jamais il n'insiste, ne charge'* (He shows good manners . . . He never works himself into a passion, never insists nor exaggerates). (The modern reader may find this last point difficult to accept, but he or she has probably

never been exposed to a French Romantic poet in full cry.)

Baudelaire certainly did not despise rhetoric; indeed in one poem (84) he tells the reader that unless he has completed the year of rhetoric in Satan's school he had better not meddle with Les Fleurs du Mal at all. (No apology is needed for calling the reader of the poem 'he', for no mid-nineteenth-century girl would have had the opportunity to faire sa rhétorique, that is, of completing the penultimate year in a lycée.) But the rhetoric that Baudelaire admires and deploys is a far subtler affair, made of figures and often of ironies. He addresses his reader in the opening poem ('Au lecteur'), only to turn on him at the end and call him a hypocrite. The later prefatory poem 'Epigraphe pour un livre condamné' addresses a 'peaceful and bucolic' reader (a type of person very unlikely to be reading Les Fleurs du Mal in the first place), and ends on a note of imperious self-absorption which reads suspiciously like a parody of the conventional Romantic stance.

The paradoxical combination of distance and intimacy that we find in Baudelaire also has a great deal to do with the way his poems unfold. Their organizing principle is often not the logic of prose discourse but a free association of ideas and memories which seemed baffling to many of those who first tried to read him. There is little overt attempt to convince the reader or explain points to him using carefully marshalled metaphors. (The famous concluding stanza of 'L'Albatros' is in fact very unusual in this respect.) The persuasive voice, when it is present, is more usually directed at some other imagined listener, a being absent at the moment of reading (a mistress, God, a cat, the poet's own heart or soul), and the flesh-and-blood reader seems not so much to hear as to overhear the poems. We bring to them our own memories and feelings, and construct a response which is no doubt peculiar to each reader.

Remarks in his correspondence and theoretical writing make it clear that Baudelaire wished to be read in this way:

the words *suggérer* and *suggestion* recur in his accounts of how good poetry works. (Painting and music, he thought, worked in similar ways.) To take one example, in his letter to Victor Hugo accompanying the dedication of 'Le Cygne' (53) he said that his chief concern in the poem had been to set down quickly '*tout ce qu'un accident, une image, peut contenir de suggestions*' (all that an accidental occurrence, an image, can give rise to by way of suggestions). This phrase is no doubt too self-disparaging – the poem in fact gives clear signs of slow and careful composition – but it is nevertheless a clue to how the poem functions.

If we believe the story as unfolded in the poem, the experience of crossing the new Place du Carrousel (a piece of triumphalist town planning built on the ruins of a picturesque old neighbourhood where poet friends of Baudelaire had lived in happier times) triggered off in his mind the memory of having seen there, one morning when the work was half completed, a swan lost among the dust and rubble, and this memory is deeply intertwined with poetic memories of An-dromache, the widow of Hector, as she is described in Virgil (*Aeneid*, III, 294–348). This twin, involuntary memory gives rise to other associations of ideas which spread in wider ripples as the poem moves to its deliberately inconclusive ending. But we would be naïve to think that the poem is a kind of stenographic record of the memories in the order in which they occurred to Baudelaire. It has an artful structure, moving from Andromache slowly to the swan, quickly back to Andromache, abruptly to the negress (a new figure in the poem), and then outwards in circles to the unspecified '*bien d'autres encor*'. It is not simply a record of one set of sugges-tions, but is designed to prompt new ones, perhaps in the poet himself and those close to him (his mother, after a second marriage he regarded as unworthy, had recently been wid-owed for the second time; his mistress of fourteen years, the person whom after his mother he probably loved most, was a

woman of mixed race from the French West Indies) or in
Victor Hugo, himself living in exile at the time he received
the poem, or, most importantly for us, in future readers
whom Baudelaire knew he would never see.

This wonderful poem is a perfect example of Laforgue's
'*façon noble, lointaine, supérieure*' – some of its lines have the
stately plangency of Racine himself – but it is also a striking
instance of Baudelaire's creative breaking of decorum in its
mixtures of décor, objects and language. We find An-
dromache's palace cheek by jowl with a building site, a cold
Paris morning with a sudden view of the coconut palms of
Africa. The human sympathy so clearly displayed in the poem
is, to prejudiced nineteenth-century eyes, extended to an un-
likely and perhaps even distasteful assortment of beings: a swan,
but not a stately swan gliding over a lake – that traditional
symbol of the poet – instead a lost creature waddling over
city paving-stones; exiles (perhaps political exiles after 1848
and 1851); orphans, shipwrecked sailors, a negress! What
could Virgil's Andromache have to do in such company?

Another thing that gives Baudelaire's verse its distant, noble
sound is the survival, or revival, in it of some dated features
of poetic language. We have seen how he abhorred the
euphemistic, circumlocutory approach of much eighteenth-
century diction, but he had a nostalgic fondness for other
aspects of eighteenth-century style. He had lived as a small child
in a flat filled with eighteenth-century furniture, pictures and
ornaments, and notes in his journal the emotional resonances
such objects still have for him. In 46 he compares the interior
of his mind to '*un vieux boudoir plein de roses fanées*', an old
boudoir full of withered roses, where once-fashionable dresses
lie in heaps, watched over only by pastel portraits and faded
Boucher prints. Some of this nostalgia perhaps underlies his
use of strikingly artificial, dated figures like personification,
complete with capital letters, and allegory. These are particu-

larly arresting when combined with gratingly modern elements, as in 'La Prostitution s'allume dans les rues' (57). Less showy and more moving is 'Recueillement' (89). In this sonnet Sorrow, the Evening, Pleasure and Regret, the Sun and Night are all capitalized, but represented in attitudes which eighteenth-century personification would hardly recognize: Regret rising from the waters like a smiling ghost, the Sun settling down to sleep under the arch of a bridge like a Parisian *clochard* and the dead Years leaning out from the balconies of heaven, dressed once more *'en robes surannées'*. Certain mannered inversions, excessively *précieux* compliments and the occasional reappearance of *style noble* words may also betray a wish to give, perhaps ironically, an eighteenth-century colouring to his style. Those who know French well will also detect in it some echoes of sixteenth- and seventeenth-century poetry which was just beginning to be read again after having been dismissed as barbarous in the classical period. Baudelaire was particularly attracted to the poetic form of the emblem; poems 68 and 90 are based on engraved emblems by Goltzius (1558–1617), deliberately misinterpreted.

No ironic intention is apparent, however, in 'Le Cygne', where some lines attain a genuine grandeur, in turn made more poignant by juxtaposition with other phrases in a much plainer style ('. . . *ce petit fleuve/ Pauvre et triste miroir où jadis resplendit/ L'immense majesté de vos douleurs de veuve'*). What is at work here is not simply contrasts of vocabulary (*petit, pauvre, triste/ resplendit, immense, majesté*) but a mastery of all the resources of French verse. It is at these technical resources that we must now briefly look.

Despite the modernity of his subject-matter and approach, Baudelaire never departed from the rules of French versification first laid down in the seventeenth century. In the same article in which he damned him with patronizing praise,

likening *Les Fleurs du Mal* to an architectural folly, a '*singulier kiosque*' built at the '*pointe extrême du Kamtschatka romantique*', the influential critic Sainte-Beuve had to recognize that he remained '*tout à fait classique dans les formes*'. This scrupulous formalism may have been related to Baudelaire's well-documented fastidiousness about dress and self-presentation; certainly Laforgue makes this analogy: '*Il peut être cynique, fou, etc. . . . jamais il n'a un pli canaille, un faux pli aux expressions dont il se vêt*' (He can be shameless, mad, etc. . . . there is never a vulgar fold, a wrong crease in the expressions in which he clothes himself). But Baudelaire seems also to have believed in the inherent suggestive power of correctly made verses. As a boy of sixteen he had come second in the Latin verse competition open to all *lycée* students, and in one of the projected prefaces to *Les Fleurs du Mal* he wrote that poetry resembled music by virtue of prosody, which sank its roots deeper into the human soul than any classical theory had yet explained. He went on to say that French verse, like Latin and English, had '*une prosodie mystérieuse et méconnue*' (a mysterious and unrecognized prosody) which, correctly used, could make the poetic phrase soar, glide, plunge, sway or zigzag. He does not say how this is to be done, but one guesses that the secret lies in rhythmical variation and careful phonetic patterning within the lines. We know that he devoted great attention to these aspects of verse-making in his many revisions of his poems.

The surface rules of French poetry, though strict, are simple, and certainly do not account for all the metrical effects that can be achieved in the language. French lines are not counted in feet, like Latin or English, but in syllables. The commonest metre, the alexandrine, must have twelve syllables in every line, no more and no less; the so-called mute *e* which most often occurs at the end of a word, and is not pronounced in modern speech in Paris and northern France, must be counted when it appears before a following consonant, and should be lightly sounded when reading verse aloud. It is not sounded

before a following vowel, or when it appears at the end of a line. The first two words of *Les Fleurs du Mal*, therefore, *la sottise*, are to be counted as four syllables and not, as they would be in modern Parisian speech, three. There are numerous minor rules about syllable counting which the interested reader will find summarized in the appendix to C. Scott's *A Question of Syllables*. But the point to be remembered is that lines of French poetry unfold in the ear of the practised listener as a succession of fixed numbers of syllables, any departure from which will be perceived as a solecism. Baudelaire's was certainly such an ear; we find him in March 1866, when already paralysed and incapable of writing, dictating a letter to his friend Prarond thanking him for a new volume of verses, praising it but calling his attention to a fault of prosody in one line.

The textbook rules, though extremely detailed about syllable counting, have remarkably little to say about rhythm, which may therefore be Baudelaire's *prosodie méconnue*. Each line of ten syllables or more is supposed to have a slight break, the caesura, which in theory occurs at the mid-point, that is, after the sixth syllable of an alexandrine. But even the classical dramatists of the seventeenth century break this rule, for a long succession of alexandrines all split in the middle produces a very tedious effect. The caesura can therefore be displaced and occur, say, after the fourth or eighth syllable, for variety or emphasis. A line split into three groups of four syllables, like the opening line of 'Le Cygne', is sometimes called a Romantic trimeter.

An English-speaking reader is surprised to find that there are no explicit rules about the distribution of stresses within the line. This is no doubt because there is less tonic stress in spoken French than in English: the stressed (that is, louder) syllables in French speech are not pronounced very much louder than the unstressed. But variations in stress are there, and stress patterns (something like musical beats) can be heard

by anyone listening to French verse read aloud. Baudelaire is a master of the rhythmical effects introduced by varying the position of the caesura and ordering the pattern of stresses in the line.

The reader can become aware of the musical aspect of Baudelaire's poetry by listening to recordings of his verse; some of those available at present are listed in the suggestions for further reading. A problem, though, is that such recordings tend to be made by actors, who are apt to perform the poems in dramatic style rather than use the more neutral delivery which would allow Baudelaire's sonorities to speak for themselves. A contemporary describes the young Baudelaire reciting his own verses in this way: '*il nous disait, ou plutôt nous psalmodiait ses vers d'une voix monotone, mais impérieuse . . .*' (he spoke, or rather intoned his verses to us in a monotonous but compelling voice . . .). The many musical settings which exist of poems by Baudelaire of course substitute their own melodies and rhythms for those of the verse, but sometimes succeed very well in capturing the mood of the originals.

Rhyming in French poetry is also bound by rules much stricter than in English. In general, rhyme plays a more conspicuous part in overall poetic effect, no doubt because French tonic stress, such as it is, always falls on the last syllable of a word, making the last syllable of every line a stressed syllable. Rhyming in French, an English-speaking person might think, must be extremely easy, given all the verbs that end in -*er* and -*ir*, and all the participles that end in -*é*, -*i*, -*u*, and -*ant*. But such easy effects are in fact avoided. A rhyme based on a single sound, as in English bay/day, is to French ideas not a rhyme at all. For a full rhyme at least two sounds must coincide (bait/date, bray/dray, *fleuve/veuve*) and rhymes where three or more elements coincide (*rime riche*) are particularly sought after. Finding rhymes has always been a struggle even for the most accomplished French poets, and Baudelaire

refers several times to their search. In his essay 'Du Vin et du Haschisch' he speaks of rag-pickers 'stumbling over the paving-stones, like young poets who spend their whole day wandering and hunting for rhymes', while in the poem 'Le Soleil' in *Les Fleurs du Mal* he describes himself in a deserted city under the cruel sun of high summer, practising

. . . ma fantasque escrime,
Flairant dans tous les coins les hasards de la rime,
Trébuchant sur les mots comme sur les pavés
Heurtant parfois des vers depuis longtemps rêvés.

[. . . practising my fantastical fencing skills, scenting in every corner the chances of rhyme, tripping over words like paving-stones, sometimes bumping into lines I had long dreamed of.]

The rhyme *escrime/rime* occurs more than once in Baudelaire's verse, and the reason no doubt is that *escrime* is one of the few 'rich' (three-element) rhymes the French language affords for *rime*. Another happy example of the 'chances of rhyme' is the lack of rich rhymes for *soir* (evening). Those that there are come almost exclusively from the realm of the liturgical: *encensoir* (thurible), *ostensoir* (monstrance) and *reposoir* (altar of repose). The whole religious (or religiose) atmosphere of 'Harmonie du Soir' (33) comes from these 'found' rhymes.

Did not Baudelaire resent the arbitrary power exerted over his writing by the demands of rhyme? It seems that he did not. In the same draft preface to *Les Fleurs du Mal* that we quoted before, he grandly states that '. . . *tout poète qui ne sait pas au juste combien chaque mot comporte de rimes est incapable d'exprimer une idée quelconque*' (. . . any poet who does not know exactly how many rhymes are available for each word is incapable of expressing the simplest idea).

For whatever reason, Baudelaire wrote little verse after 1862

and the project on which he was engaged when he became hopelessly ill was a book of prose poems (then a very novel idea; the very title *Petits Poëmes en prose* appeared deliberately paradoxical). This new departure would have posed radical new problems of organization and formal character. Certainly, Baudelaire did not intend simply to write pieces of everyday, discursive or journalistic prose. His ideal, as he expressed it in the preface to *Le Spleen de Paris*, was

le miracle d'une prose poétique, musicale sans rythme et sans rime, assez souple et assez heurtée pour s'adapter aux mouvements lyriques de l'âme, aux ondulations de la rêverie, aux soubresauts de la conscience.

[the miracle of a poetic prose, musical without fixed rhythm or rhyme, flexible and irregular enough to match the lyrical movements of the soul, the wave-motions of dream, the sudden starts of consciousness.]

Critics have disagreed about the meaning of these expressions and whether or not Baudelaire achieved this desired new form in his lifetime. What is clear, however, is that at every period of his life he attached the greatest importance to formal mastery in writing, and saw it as perfectly compatible with originality. As he himself wrote in his review of the annual Salon exhibition of painting in 1859:

il est évident que les rhétoriques et les prosodies ne sont pas des tyrannies inventées arbitrairement, mais une collection de règles réclamées par l'organisation même de l'être spirituel. Et jamais les prosodies et les rhétoriques n'ont empêché l'originalité de se produire distinctement. Le contraire, à savoir qu'elles ont aidé l'éclosion de l'originalité, serait infiniment plus vrai.

[it is evident that rhetorics and prosodies are not arbitrarily invented tyrannies, but a collection of rules required by the very organization

of the spiritual being. And prosodies and rhetorics have never stopped originality from making itself clearly apparent. The opposite, that is, that they have helped originality to blossom, would be infinitely more true.]

This translation does not pretend to be anything but an aid to reading the poems in French. It does not (and, I believe, could not) aspire to convey the rhythms and melody of the originals, but at most to avoid outright cacophony. To help the reader whose French is not strong, I have followed wherever possible the grammatical constructions of the original; where I have not, it is because I judged the order in which words appear in a line more important than the precise syntax.

Baudelaire's own definition of *une poésie bien faite*, a well-made poem, was that it should be

... explicative par elle-même, tant toutes choses y sont bien unies, conjointes, réciproquement adaptées, et [...] prudemment *concaténées*.

[self-explanatory, so well joined and brought together are all its elements, so matched to each other and carefully *concatenated*.]

The reader of such a poem, in my view, should not be constantly distracted by biographical or speculative editorial notes. Baudelaire was also fanatically particular about the look of his poems on the printed page; I cannot believe that it would have given him pleasure to see them pock-marked with superscript numbers. The modern reader, however, does need some additional factual information if he or she does not have immediate access to reference books. Baudelaire is not a learned poet, but he takes for granted the classical and literary knowledge which his original readers, predominantly men of the middle or upper class with a *lycée* education, would have had. Not all modern readers have such knowledge, and I have

tried to supply the want with a glossary of proper names and foreign phrases.

I have tried as far as possible to translate each word by a word of similar register; the incongruities to which this sometimes gives rise are, in general, present in the original also. In Baudelaire's lines there are quite often echoes of other kinds of discourse, notably religious but sometimes, for example, journalistic, and these I have tried to keep. Echoes of the Bible and the Prayer Book are intentional.

There are, however, certain characteristics of Baudelaire's language, and of the French language in general, that cannot be translated into English. One is word order: the poet's *blanche maison* is not the same as a *maison blanche* or the swan's *blanc plumage* as a *plumage blanc*. Still more important is the availability of two words for 'you', *tu* and *vous*. We are told at school that *vous* is polite and *tu* familiar, but the truth is much more complex. *Vous*, in Baudelaire's time, was the form used in writing and public speech between all adults of the middle class and above; even husbands and wives of this class called each other and their children above infancy *vous*. *Tu* was reserved for private speech; in public it was only used to small children, animals and people of definitely lower class; polite people called even servants, waiters and the like *vous*. For a man to call a woman of his own class *tu* would have indicated a sexual relationship between them. This is brought out very clearly in a letter from Baudelaire to Madame Sabatier (the dedicatee of poems 27–32), written on 31 August 1857. Previously he had always addressed her as *vous*; in this letter, written after they had spent the night together for the first and only time, he fluctuates between *tu* and *vous*, eventually settling for *vous*, which he uses in all subsequent correspondence.

The tone of the love poems in 'Spleen et Idéal' is strongly influenced by the form of address used: poems XXII to XXXIX (our 13–26) with the exception of 'Une Charogne' use *tu*, XL

to XLV (our 27–31) *vous*, XLVI to LIV (our 32–9) use *tu* again, while LV to LXIV (our 40–43) vary according to no discernible pattern. There is no way of rendering this distinction in English.

But the problem does not end here. As well as the *tu* used to children and mistresses, there is the *tu* used in prayer. French Catholics of this period, and for a hundred years afterwards, did most of their praying in Latin; Protestants had prayed in French since the sixteenth century. Latin prayers address God in the singular, *tu*, and this practice is followed in French in the sixteenth and seventeenth centuries. Thus Protestants, using a sixteenth-century translation, have always prayed '*Notre père, qui es aux cieux . . .*' and Racine's devotional poetry uses *tu* to God. By the nineteenth century, however, this was considered undignified, and Catholics prayed '*Notre Père, qui êtes . . .*' However it was not unknown for God the Father to be called *tu* in poetry and Jesus was regularly so addressed. The Virgin Mary, on the other hand, was usually called *vous*, no doubt because of the disrespect implied by using *tu* to a woman. The *Ave Maria* was, and is, always rendered '*Je vous salue, Marie . . .*' (Protestants of course do not pray to the Virgin.) Baudelaire uses *vous* to God the Father (67), but *tu* to Jesus (69), Satan (71) and the Madone addressed in 41. I have used Prayer Book 'thee' and 'thou' in 71, as suiting the deliberate perversity of the piece, but not in 69, where the stress is on the vulnerable humanity of Jesus. I was tempted to use it in 41, but felt that I would thereby have lost the mixture of perversity and intimacy in a poem addressed to a woman whose own name was Marie.

Grevisse's *Le Bon Usage*, the bible of French usage, states with no apparent sense of incongruity that

Tu, te, toi et les possessifs correspondants expriment l'intimité, la supériorité, l'arrogance ou le dédain. Ils peuvent aussi prendre un caractère pathétique ou noble.

[*Tu*, *te*, *toi* and the corresponding possessive adjectives express intimacy, social superiority, arrogance or disdain. They can also take on an emotional or elevated (i.e. conventionally poetic) character.]

Clearly this grammatical form is highly suited to addressing someone who is thought of at the same time as a child and a mistress, a goddess and a frail woman, a fallen angel and a protective divinity, a God and a broken man. But English has no *tu*.

French speech and writing is also affected by grammatical gender. All nouns in French, including the names of objects and abstractions, are either masculine or feminine; there is no grammatical neuter, no 'it' but only 'he' and 'she'. Most abstractions are in fact feminine (*la Nature, la Beauté, la Mort*) and this makes it natural for French poets, when personifying them, to give them the characteristics traditionally regarded as feminine. Baudelaire does seem to go further, however, when he personifies Beauty as a flirtatious female using her eyes to fascinate her docile lovers (9) or, in 65, Debauchery and Death as two good-hearted girls ('*deux aimables filles*' – but *fille* had the meaning 'prostitute' as well as 'girl' at this period). Beauty's first words, in 9, 'Je suis belle, ô mortels', make it clear, simply by the form *belle*, that a feminine character is speaking, in a way that English cannot do.

Less stereotyped and more affecting is the way in which, in 89, Baudelaire addresses his Sorrow (*ma Douleur*) in a patient, gentle voice as if coaxing a little girl, or, very strikingly, in 31, figures the note he suddenly hears in his mistress's voice (*la note*) as an unloved girl-child hidden away by her family and singing a song of despairing resignation.

The reverse process seems to be at work when the old women of 'Les Petites Vieilles' (55), unsexed by age, are first called '*des êtres*' (beings) and '*des monstres*', both masculine nouns; grammar requires that they should then for the next four stanzas be called *ils* and not *elles*, and that any adjective

applying to them (*brisés, bossus, tordus, cassés*: broken, hunch-backed, twisted, crippled) should be in the masculine and not the feminine form. This is poetically most appropriate to the opening section of the poem, where the reader's attention is first directed towards the strange, barely human aspect of these still living creatures; as the poem develops and human sympathy, understanding, and even love are expressed for them, they are allowed once more to take on their appropriate gender.

In Baudelaire's own, chosen poetic vocabulary the chief problem for the translator is a group of short, extremely simple words that recur with great frequency, several of which cover a whole range of English meanings. French is not, in general, a monosyllabic language, but of the forty most often repeated words in 'Spleen et Idéal' no fewer than sixteen are monosyllables, and another three (*âme, ange, charme*) would be counted as monosyllables in everyday speech but count as disyllables in certain verse contexts. The sixteen 'true' monosyllables (by the rules of French metre) are all either open syllables or end in 'r' and it is nearly impossible to render them by anything so phonetically unobtrusive. How is one to translate the endlessly recurring *beau* (fair, fine, beautiful?), *grand* (great, grand, large?), *doux* (sweet, soft, gentle, quiet?)? The worst nightmare is *ivre*, which when it does not mean drunk, and it usually does not, has the translator hesitating between 'high' (too slangy) and the impossibly prissy 'intoxicated'. 'Intoxication' for *ivresse* is dreadful, but 'rapture' makes one think of the hymn-book or of Elinor Glyn. Even *mal* is a problem, for it means both 'evil' and 'sickness'.

Baudelaire wrote that '*Manier savamment une langue, c'est pratiquer une espèce de sorcellerie évocatoire*' (to use a language with superior knowledge and skill is to practise a kind of conjuring). Conjuring in the strong sense, that of calling up

visions or spirits. A plain prose translation can never have such powers, but must simply try to put the reader in touch with the magical original.

NOTES ON THE TEXT

Of the ninety-three verse poems printed here, ninety-one come from *Les Fleurs du Mal*. This collection, first printed in 1857 in an edition of 1,100 copies, contains all but a very few of Baudelaire's poems in verse. A good many of them had appeared previously in magazines, some as early as 1850–51. On publication, *Les Fleurs du Mal* was the subject of a prosecution for offence against public decency and the court required that six poems should be expunged before any copies were put on sale. These six poems were finally published in 1866 in Belgium, together with some other short pieces, to make a pamphlet called *Les Epaves*, which was printed in 260 copies. In 1861 a second edition of *Les Fleurs du Mal* appeared, still missing the six banned poems, but including thirty-five previously unpublished ones. Like the first edition, it is organized in sections, but some poems have been moved from one section to another and an important new section has been created, the 'Tableaux parisiens'. This edition, the last to appear in the author's lifetime, is the one usually followed in modern French texts of Baudelaire.

A third edition appeared in 1868 as Volume I of Baudelaire's complete works: it included some previously unpublished poems, not all of them obviously intended for *Les Fleurs du Mal*.

The poems printed here are taken from the text, and printed in the order, of 1861, up to 'Le Voyage'. As well as our own numbers, we have given in brackets the number of each poem in the original (1861) edition, so as to make it easier for the reader to locate poems in a French text. The

remaining poems are taken from *Les Epaves* and the edition of 1868; here the sections are short and the numbering varies from one modern French text to another, so we have given only our own numbers.

The *Petits Poëmes en prose* (for which Baudelaire's working title was *Le Spleen de Paris*) first appeared separately in magazines between 1855 and 1867. The first collected edition, including a further five previously unpublished poems, was in Volume V of the *Œuvres complètes*, in 1869. Our selections follow the text and give the numbering of this edition.

SUGGESTIONS FOR FURTHER READING

WRITINGS BY BAUDELAIRE

Œuvres complètes, edited by Claude Pichois, 2 vols. (Paris, Gallimard, Editions de la Pléiade, 1975 and 1976)

Les Fleurs du Mal, edited by Jacques Dupont (Paris, Garnier-Flammarion, 1991)

Le Spleen de Paris and *La Fanfarlo*, edited by David Scott and Barbara Wright (Paris, Garnier-Flammarion, 1987)

TRANSLATIONS

Baudelaire, *Volume I: The Complete Verse* and *Volume II: The Complete Prose*, with introductions and translations by Francis Scarfe (London, Anvil Press Poetry, 1986)

Baudelaire as a Literary Critic. Selected essays introduced and translated by Lois Boe Hyslop and Francis E. Hyslop Jr (Pennsylvania State University Press, 1964)

Flowers of Evil and Other Works, edited and translated by Wallace Fowlie (New York, 1964; reprinted London, Dover Books, 1992)

Intimate Journals, translated by Christopher Isherwood with an introduction by T. S. Eliot (1930; reprinted London, Black Spring, 1989)

Selected Letters of Charles Baudelaire, translated and edited by Rosemary Lloyd (London, Weidenfeld & Nicolson, 1986)

My Heart Laid Bare and Other Prose Writings, translated by Norman Cameron with an introduction by Peter Quennell (London, Weidenfeld & Nicolson, 1950; reprinted London, Soho Book Company, 1986)

The Prose Poems and La Fanfarlo, translated with an introduc-

tion by Rosemary Lloyd (Oxford, Oxford University Press, The World's Classics, 1991)

Selected Writings on Art and Literature, translated by P. E. Charvet (London, Penguin Books, 1972)

BIOGRAPHICAL STUDIES

Hemmings, F. W. J., *Baudelaire the Damned: A Biography* (New York, Scribner, 1982)

Lloyd, R., *Baudelaire's World* (Bloomington, IN, Cornell University Press, 2002)

Pichois, C., with additional research by J. Ziegler, abridged and translated by G. Robb, *Baudelaire* (London, Hamish Hamilton, 1989)

Starkie, E., *Baudelaire* (London, Faber & Faber, 1957; Penguin Books, 1971)

Sartre, J.-P., *Baudelaire* (Paris, 1947)

CRITICAL STUDIES

Benjamin, W., *Charles Baudelaire: A Lyric Poet in the Era of High Capitalism* (1935, 1939, 1955; translated from the German by H. Zohn, London, Verso, 1983)

Burton, R., *Baudelaire in 1859: A Study in Poetic Creativity* (Cambridge, Cambridge University Press, 1989)

Chesters, G., *Baudelaire and the Poetics of Craft* (Cambridge, Cambridge University Press, 1988)

Fairlie, A., *Baudelaire: Les Fleurs du Mal* (London, Arnold, 1960)

Fairlie, A., *Imagination and Language*, edited by M. Bowie (Cambridge, Cambridge University Press, 1979)

Hiddleston, J., *Baudelaire and Le Spleen de Paris* (Oxford, Clarendon Press, 1986)

Laforgue, J., 'Notes sur Baudelaire', in *Mélanges posthumes*, edited by Ph. Bonnefis (Geneva, Slatkine, 1979)

Leakey, F. W., *Baudelaire: Les Fleurs du Mal* (Cambridge, Cambridge University Press, Landmarks in World Literature, 1992)

Proust, Marcel, 'Concerning Baudelaire', in *Against Sainte-Beuve and Other Essays*, translated by John Sturrock (Penguin Books 1988)

BACKGROUND AND GENERAL CRITICISM

Broome, J. P., and Chesters, G., *The Appreciation of Modern French Poetry* (Cambridge, Cambridge University Press, 1976)

Gibson, R., *Modern French Poets on Poetry: An Anthology* (Cambridge, Cambridge University Press, 1961, 1979)

Lewis, R., *On Reading French Verse: A Study of Poetic Form* (Oxford, Clarendon Press, 1982)

Lough, J. G., and Lough, M., *An Introduction to Nineteenth Century France* (London, Longman, 1978)

Praz, M., *The Romantic Agony* (London, Oxford University Press, 1933; 2nd edn, 1951, 1970)

Prendergast, C., *Paris and the Nineteenth Century* (Oxford, Blackwell, 1992)

Prendergast, C., ed., *Nineteenth Century French Poetry: Introductions to Close Reading* (Cambridge, Cambridge University Press, 1990)

Scott, C., *A Question of Syllables: Essays in Nineteenth-century French Verse* (Cambridge, Cambridge University Press, 1986)

RECORDINGS

Les Fleurs du Mal: les pages qu'il faut connaître, lu par Pierre Blanchar (Paris, Hachette, L'Encyclopédie sonore)

Charles Baudelaire dit par Jean Dessailly, avec la participation de Denis Manuel et Jean Vilar (Paris, Adès, 1976)

Baudelaire, Les Fleurs du Mal dites par Alain Moussay (texte intégral) (Paris, Claudine Ducaté Éditions, 1991)

Les Fleurs du Mal, textes intégraux dits par Jacques Roland (Périgord, Le Livre qui parle, 1990)

CHRONOLOGY

1821 *9 April*: Charles Pierre Baudelaire is born at 13, rue Hautefeuille, Paris.

1827 *10 February*: his father dies, aged sixty-seven.

1828 His mother remarries. Her new husband, Commandant Aupick, is thirty-nine.

1833 Baudelaire is sent as a boarder to the Collège Royal at Lyon, where the family has moved on Commandant Aupick's promotion to lieutenant-colonel.

1836 The family returns to Paris. Baudelaire now boards at the Collège Louis-le-Grand.

1839 Expelled from Louis-le-Grand for disciplinary offences. Baudelaire continues to work for the baccalaureate at a private coaching establishment in the Latin Quarter, and passes it in August.

1841 Living in rooms in Paris, Baudelaire is beginning to make friendships in the literary world. His irregular lifestyle alarms his parents and they send him on a long sea voyage to India.

1842 On his return to Paris, he resumes his literary lifestyle, living for a time on the Ile St-Louis and making friends of Theophile Gautier and Theodore de Banville. Begins what was to be a lifetime affair with Jeanne Duval (or Prosper or Lemer), a bit-part actress in small theatres.

1844 At his mother's request, Baudelaire's finances are put under the permanent control of a lawyer (a '*conseil judiciare*').

1845 First published works: 'Salon de 1845', a poem and a short article on Balzac. After a suicide attempt on 30 June, Baudelaire returns to live in the house of his stepfather, now General Aupick, at the prestigious address of 7, place

Vendôme. After a few weeks, however, he moves out again, to a furnished room.

1846 Publishes 'Salon de 1846' and some poems.

1847 Publishes 'La Fanfarlo' and some poems. His portrait by Courbet is refused by the Salon.

1848 Confused involvement in the revolution of that year. Publishes in both left- and right-wing papers. Accepts the editorship of a right-wing paper published in a small provincial town, then returns to Paris a week later. General Aupick is appointed ambassador to Constantinople.

1850 Frequent changes of address, journalism, some poems published in magazines.

1851 General Aupick appointed ambassador to Madrid. Coup d'état: Louis Napoleon Bonaparte becomes Emperor Napoleon III.

1852 Baudelaire publishes a critical essay on Poe (the first in France) in the important *Revue de Paris*, and begins to publish translations of Poe's tales and essays. His obsession with Mme Sabatier, a beautiful and intelligent *demi-mondaine*, begins. In December he sends her, anonymously, the first of a series of poems.

1853 Publishes more translations of Poe, sends more poems to Mme Sabatier. General Aupick is appointed to the Senate and he and his wife return to Paris.

1854 Magazine publication of his complete translation of Poe's tales between July 1854 and April 1855. Friendship with the successful actress Marie Daubrun, but intermittent cohabitation with Jeanne Duval and anonymous poetic courtship of Mme Sabatier continue.

1855 Constant moves: six changes of address between March and April.
1 June: the *Revue des Deux Mondes* (a highly regarded journal) publishes eighteen of Baudelaire's poems under the name *Les Fleurs du Mal*: the first appearance of this title.

1856 Publication in book form of Poe's *Histoires Extraordinaires*.

1857 *28 April*: death of General Aupick. His wife retires to the seaside at Honfleur.

25 June: publication of *Les Fleurs du Mal* (cover price 3 francs).

5 July: violently hostile review in *Le Figaro*.

16 July: the edition is impounded and the author and publishers charged with an offence against public morals.

20 August: guilty verdict, Baudelaire is fined 300 francs. The book can only be put on sale again if six poems are physically removed.

24 August: publication of Baudelaire's first prose poems.

31 August: ending of his relationship with Mme Sabatier.

1858 Health difficulties. Magazine publication of some poems and essays.

1859 Baudelaire spends several highly productive periods at his mother's house at Honfleur, and speaks of going to live there permanently. At the same time, he lives intermittently with Jeanne Duval in Paris. Publication of several important articles and poems.

1860 Publication in book form of *Les Paradis Artificiels* (Baudelaire's essays on wine, hashish and opium) and, in magazines, of further poems including 'Le Cygne'.

1861 Second edition of *Les Fleurs du Mal*, including thirty-five new poems. Baudelaire stands, unsuccessfully, for election to the Académie Française.

1862–3 Magazine publication of poems, essays, translations, art criticism.

1864–5 Six prose poems published in *Le Figaro*.

24 April: Baudelaire travels to Brussels to give a series of lectures and to negotiate with Belgian publishers. None of his initiatives is successful and his health is failing. Apart from a brief trip back to Paris and Honfleur in July 1865, he remains in Belgium, avoiding his French creditors.

1866 *March*: collapses in the church of St-Loup at Namur. From then on his health deteriorates rapidly: one side of his

body is paralysed and he progressively loses the power of speech.

April: his friend and publisher Poulet-Malassis brings out a slim volume, *Les Epaves*, which includes the six poems excised from *Les Fleurs du Mal*, and a further seventeen new poems, with a frontispiece by Félicien Rops.

July: Baudelaire is brought back to Paris, accompanied by his mother, and placed in a clinic.

1867 *31 August*: Baudelaire dies. He is buried in the Cimetière Montparnasse, in the grave bought ten years before for General Aupick. The gravestone describes him as the general and ambassador's stepson, making no mention of his literary career. As Baudelaire died intestate, a relative on his father's side claims his estate, and the rights to his entire work are sold at auction in December 1867, fetching 1,750 francs.

1868 Publication of the *Petits Poèmes en Prose* and the final edition of *Les Fleurs du Mal*. *Les Epaves* is banned by the Belgian courts and all surviving copies are ordered to be destroyed. Poulet-Malassis is condemned in absentia to a year in jail and a 500-franc fine.

1871 *16 August*: Mme Aupick dies and is buried in the family grave. Her inscription describes her as the general's widow and 'mère de Charles Baudelaire'.

LES FLEURS DU MAL

(Flowers of Evil)

1 Au Lecteur

La sottise, l'erreur, le péché, la lésine,
Occupent nos esprits et travaillent nos corps,
Et nous alimentons nos aimables remords,
Comme les mendiants nourrissent leur vermine.

Nos péchés sont têtus, nos repentirs sont lâches;
Nous nous faisons payer grassement nos aveux,
Et nous rentrons gaiement dans le chemin bourbeux,
Croyant par de vils pleurs laver toutes nos taches.

Sur l'oreiller du mal c'est Satan Trismégiste
Qui berce longuement notre esprit enchanté,
Et le riche métal de notre volonté
Est tout vaporisé par ce savant chimiste.

....

To the Reader

Stupidity, error, sin, meanness fill up our minds and work upon our bodies,
and we keep our dear pangs of remorse well fed, as beggars support their
vermin.

Our sins are stubborn, our moments of repentance feeble; we demand a
fat reward for our confessions, and set out cheerfully again on the muddy
path, thinking to wash away all our stains with cheap tears.

On the pillow of evil it is thrice-great Satan who keeps our bewitched
spirit long slumbering, and the rich metal of our will-power is all turned to
vapour by that master of chemistry.

C'est le Diable qui tient les fils qui nous remuent!
Aux objets répugnants nous trouvons des appas;
Chaque jour vers l'Enfer nous descendons d'un pas,
Sans horreur, à travers des ténèbres qui puent.

Ainsi qu'un débauché pauvre qui baise et mange
Le sein martyrisé d'une antique catin,
Nous volons au passage un plaisir clandestin
Que nous pressons bien fort comme une vieille orange.

Serré, fourmillant, comme un million d'helminthes,
Dans nos cerveaux ribote un peuple de Démons,
Et, quand nous respirons, la Mort dans nos poumons
Descend, fleuve invisible, avec de sourdes plaintes.

Si le viol, le poison, le poignard, l'incendie,
N'ont pas encor brodé de leurs plaisants dessins
Le canevas banal de nos piteux destins,
C'est que notre âme, hélas! n'est pas assez hardie.

....

The strings that move us are held by the Devil! We find charm in
disgusting things; every day we go a step further down towards Hell,
without horror, through stinking darkness.

Like a penniless debauchee, kissing and gnawing the battered breast of an
ancient whore, we steal in passing some illicit pleasure, which we squeeze
very hard, like an old, dry orange.

Packed together, seething like a million intestinal worms, in our brains a
population of Demons runs riot, and when we breathe, Death, like an
invisible river, goes down into our lungs with a sound of quiet complaint.

If rope, poison, the dagger, arson have not yet embroidered their pleasing
patterns on the dull canvas of our wretched fates, it is because our souls, alas,
are not daring enough.

Mais parmi les chacals, les panthères, les lices,
Les singes, les scorpions, les vautours, les serpents,
Les monstres glapissants, hurlants, grognants, rampants,
Dans la ménagerie infâme de nos vices,

Il en est un plus laid, plus méchant, plus immonde!
Quoiqu'il ne pousse ni grands gestes ni grands cris,
Il ferait volontiers de la terre un débris
Et dans un bâillement avalerait le monde;

C'est l'Ennui! – l'œil chargé d'un pleur involontaire,
Il rêve d'échafauds en fumant son houka.
Tu le connais, lecteur, ce monstre délicat,
– Hypocrite lecteur, – mon semblable, – mon frère!

....

But among the jackals, panthers, hound bitches, monkeys, scorpions, vultures, snakes, the yelping, howling, growling, crawling monsters in the infamous menagerie of our vices,

There is one uglier, wickeder, fouler than all! He does not strike great attitudes nor utter great cries, but he would happily lay waste the earth, and swallow up the world in a yawn.

It is Boredom! – an involuntary tear welling in his eye, he dreams of scaffolds as he smokes his hookah. You know him, reader, that fastidious monster – hypocritical reader, my fellow-man, my brother!

SPLEEN ET IDÉAL

(*Spleen and the Ideal*)

2 (II) L'Albatros

Souvent, pour s'amuser, les hommes d'équipage
Prennent des albatros, vastes oiseaux des mers,
Qui suivent, indolents compagnons de voyage,
Le navire glissant sur les gouffres amers.

A peine les ont-ils déposés sur les planches,
Que ces rois de l'azur, maladroits et honteux,
Laissent piteusement leurs grandes ailes blanches
Comme des avirons traîner à côté d'eux.

Ce voyageur ailé, comme il est gauche et veule!
Lui, naguère si beau, qu'il est comique et laid!
L'un agace son bec avec un brûle-gueule,
L'autre mime, en boitant, l'infirme qui volait!

....

The Albatross

Often, for fun, crewmen catch albatrosses, huge seabirds, easy-moving travelling companions who follow the ship as it glides over the briny depths.

No sooner have they set them down on the deck, than the kings of the sky, clumsy and ashamed, drop their great white wings and let them drag piteously after them like oars.

See the winged voyager, how clumsy and feeble he is! So beautiful a moment ago, now so comical and ugly! One of them teases his beak with an old pipe, another, limping, mimics the cripple who once could fly.

Le Poète est semblable au prince des nuées
Qui hante la tempête et se rit de l'archer;
Exilé sur le sol au milieu des huées,
Ses ailes de géant l'empêchent de marcher.

3 (v)

J'aime le souvenir de ces époques nues,
Dont Phœbus se plaisait à dorer les statues.
Alors l'homme et la femme en leur agilité
Jouissaient sans mensonge et sans anxiété,
Et, le ciel amoureux leur caressant l'échine,
Exerçaient la santé de leur noble machine.
Cybèle alors, fertile en produits généreux,
Ne trouvait point ses fils un poids trop onéreux,
Mais, louve au cœur gonflé de tendresses communes,
Abreuvait l'univers à ses tétines brunes.

....

The Poet is like the prince of the clouds, who haunts the tempest and laughs at the archer. Exiled on the ground in the midst of the jeering crowd, his giant's wings keep him from walking.

3

I love to remember those nude epochs whose statues Phoebus delighted to gild. Then men and women in their agility enjoyed each other without lying and without anxiety, and, under a loving heaven which caressed their backs, deployed all the health of their noble constitution. Cybele in those days, fertile and generously productive, did not find her children too burdensome a weight, but, her she-wolf's heart swelling with general love, fed the universe at her brown dugs. Man, elegant, robust and strong, had the right to be proud of the beauties who called him their king, those fruits untouched by any

L'homme, élégant, robuste et fort, avait le droit
D'être fier des beautés qui le nommaient leur roi;
Fruits purs de tout outrage et vierges de gerçures,
Dont la chair lisse et ferme appelait les morsures!

Le Poète aujourd'hui, quand il veut concevoir
Ces natives grandeurs, aux lieux où se font voir
La nudité de l'homme et celle de la femme,
Sent un froid ténébreux envelopper son âme
Devant ce noir tableau plein d'épouvantement.
O monstruosités pleurant leur vêtement!
O ridicules troncs! torses dignes de masques!
O pauvres corps tordus, maigres, ventrus ou flasques,
Que le dieu de l'Utile, implacable et serein,
Enfants, emmaillota dans ses langes d'airain!
Et vous, femmes, hélas! pâles comme des cierges,
Que ronge et que nourrit la débauche, et vous, vierges,
Du vice maternel traînant l'hérédité
Et toutes les hideurs de la fécondité!

....

outrage and free from blemish, whose smooth, firm skin called out to be
bitten into.

The Poet today, when he tries to call up that original grandeur, in the
places where the nakedness of man and that of woman can be seen, feels a
chilling darkness envelop his soul before that black and terrifying scene. O
monstrous forms, weeping for their covering! O ridiculous trunks, torsos
worthy of masks! O poor twisted bodies, skinny, pot-bellied or flabby,
which the God of the Useful, implacable and serene, swaddled from their
infancy in bands of bronze!

And you, women, alas, pale as church candles, fed and gnawed away by
debauchery, and you, virgins, dragging along the inheritance of your
mothers' vice and all the hideous appurtenances of fecundity!

Nous avons, il est vrai, nations corrompues,
Aux peuples anciens des beautés inconnues:
Des visages rongés par les chancres du cœur,
Et comme qui dirait des beautés de langueur;
Mais ces inventions de nos muses tardives
N'empêcheront jamais les races maladives
De rendre à la jeunesse un hommage profond,
– A la sainte jeunesse, à l'air simple, au doux front,
A l'œil limpide et clair ainsi qu'une eau courante,
Et qui va répandant sur tout, insouciante
Comme l'azur du ciel, les oiseaux et les fleurs,
Ses parfums, ses chansons et ses douces chaleurs!

....

We have, it is true, we corrupt nations, beauties unknown to the ancient peoples; faces eaten away by the chancres of the heart, and, as you might say, beauties of sickness. But these inventions of our latter-day muses will never keep the sickly races from rendering a profound homage to youth, to holy youth, with its simple manners, its sweet face, its limpid eyes, clear as a running stream, which, as it goes forth, careless as the blue of the sky, the birds and the flowers, spreads over everything its scents, its songs and its own sweet warmth.

4 (VII) La Muse Malade

Ma pauvre muse, hélas! qu'as-tu donc ce matin?
Tes yeux creux sont peuplés de visions nocturnes,
Et je vois tour à tour réfléchis sur ton teint
La folie et l'horreur, froides et taciturnes.

Le succube verdâtre et le rose lutin
T'ont-ils versé la peur et l'amour de leurs urnes?
Le cauchemar, d'un poing despotique et mutin,
T'a-t-il noyée au fond d'un fabuleux Minturnes?

Je voudrais qu'exhalant l'odeur de la santé
Ton sein de pensers forts fût toujours fréquenté,
Et que ton sang chrétien coulât à flots rythmiques,

Comme les sons nombreux des syllabes antiques,
Où règnent tour à tour le père des chansons,
Phœbus, et le grand Pan, le seigneur des moissons.

....

The Sick Muse

Muse, poor darling, what is the matter with you this morning? Your hollow
eyes are full of night-time visions, and I can see reflected by turns in your
complexion madness and horror, cold and taciturn.

Have the green-skinned succubus and the pink elf poured out fear and
love for you from their urns? Has the nightmare, taking you in its despotic,
rebellious grip, forced you to the bottom of a fairy-tale swamp?

I should like to see your bosom, ever filled with strong thoughts, exhaling
the odour of health, and your Christian blood flowing with a rhythmic
pulse,

Like the measured syllables of ancient verse, in which reign by turns the
father of song, Phoebus, and great Pan, the lord of harvests.

5 (VIII) La Muse Vénale

O muse de mon cœur, amante des palais,
Auras-tu, quand Janvier lâchera ses Borées,
Durant les noirs ennuis des neigeuses soirées,
Un tison pour chauffer tes deux pieds violets?

Ranimeras-tu donc tes épaules marbrées
Aux nocturnes rayons qui percent les volets?
Sentant ta bourse à sec autant que ton palais,
Récolteras-tu l'or des voûtes azurées?

Il te faut, pour gagner ton pain de chaque soir,
Comme un enfant de chœur, jouer de l'encensoir,
Chanter des *Te Deum* auxquels tu ne crois guère,

Ou, saltimbanque à jeun, étaler tes appas
Et ton rire trempé de pleurs qu'on ne voit pas,
Pour faire épanouir la rate du vulgaire.

....

The Venal Muse

O muse of my heart, lover of palaces, when January looses its north winds,
through the long tedium of the snowy evenings, will you have a few embers
to warm your two purple feet?

Will you warm your blotched shoulders back to life in the rays of the
moon shining through the shutters? Feeling your purse as dry as your palate,
will you gather gold from the vaults of heaven?

No; to win your evening bread you will have to swing the censer like an
altar-boy and sing Te Deums in which you hardly believe,

Or, like a starving street acrobat, show off your charms and your laugh
steeped in unseen tears, all to give the public a bit of a laugh.

6 (IX) Le Mauvais Moine

Les closîtres anciens sur leurs grandes murailles
Etalaient en tableaux la sainte Vérité.
Dont l'effet, réchauffant les pieuses entrailles,
Tempérait la froideur de leur austérité.

En ces temps où du Christ florissaient les semailles,
Plus d'un illustre moine, aujourd'hui peu cité,
Prenant pour atelier le champ des funérailles,
Glorifiait la Mort avec simplicité.

— Mon âme est un tombeau que, mauvais cénobite,
Depuis l'éternité je parcours et j'habite;
Rien n'embellit les murs de ce cloître odieux.

O moine fainéant! quand saurai-je donc faire
Du spectacle vivant de ma triste misère
Le travail de mes mains et l'amour de mes yeux?

....

The Bad Monk

Ancient cloisters on their great walls displayed in paintings the sacred Truth;
the effect was to warm the bowels of the pious and temper the coldness of
their austere life.

In those times when the seeds of Christ flourished, more than one famous
monk, little mentioned nowadays, taking for his workshop the field of
burials, glorified Death with simplicity.

My soul is a tomb in which, like a bad coenobite, I have lived and moved
from all eternity; nothing beautifies the walls of that hateful cloister.

O idle monk! When shall I ever be able to make of the living spectacle of
my wretched misery the work of my hands and the love of my eyes?

7 (XI) Le Guignon

Pour soulever un poids si lourd,
Sisyphe, il faudrait ton courage!
Bien qu'on ait du cœur à l'ouvrage,
L'Art est long et le Temps est court.

Loin des sépultures célèbres,
Vers un cimetière isolé,
Mon cœur, comme un tambour voilé,
Va battant des marches funèbres.

– Maint joyau dort enseveli
Dans les ténèbres et l'oubli,
Bien loin des pioches et des sondes;

Mainte fleur épanche à regret
Son parfum doux comme un secret
Dans les solitudes profondes.

....

Bad Luck

To lift such a heavy weight, Sisyphus, a man would need your courage. Though we work with a good heart, Art is long and Time is fleeting.

Far from the tombs of the famous, towards a lonely graveyard, my heart, like a muffled drum, goes beating funeral marches.

Many a gem sleeps buried in dark forgetfulness, far, far from picks and plumb-lines;

Many a flower unwillingly looses its perfume, sweet as a secret, in deep solitudes.

8 (XII) La Vie Antérieure

J'ai longtemps habité sous de vastes portiques
Que les soleils marins teignaient de mille feux,
Et que leurs grands piliers, droits et majestueux,
Rendaient pareils, le soir, aux grottes basaltiques.

Les houles, en roulant les images des cieux,
Mêlaient d'une façon solennelle et mystique
Les tout-puissants accords de leur riche musique
Aux couleurs du couchant reflété par mes yeux.

C'est là que j'ai vécu dans les voluptés calmes,
Au milieu de l'azur, des vagues, des splendeurs
Et des esclaves nus, tout imprégnés d'odeurs,

Qui me rafraîchissaient le front avec des palmes,
Et dont l'unique soin était d'approfondir
Le secret douloureux qui me faisait languir.

....

Former Life

I lived for a long time under vast porticoes which marine suns coloured with
a thousand lights, and whose great pillars, tall and majestic, made them
look, at evening, like basalt caves.

The rolling waves, reflecting the images of the skies, mingled in a solemn
and mystic fashion the all-powerful chords of their rich music with the
colours of the sunset reflected in my eyes.

That is where I lived, amid calm pleasures, surrounded by the azure skies,
the waves, the shining lights and the naked slaves, soaked in perfumes,

Who fanned my face with palm leaves, and whose only care was to
uncover the sad secret which kept me languishing.

9 (XVII) La Beauté

Je suis belle, ô mortels! comme un rêve de pierre,
Et mon sein, où chacun s'est meurtri tour à tour,
Est fait pour inspirer au poète un amour
Eternel et muet ainsi que la matière.

Je trône dans l'azur comme un sphinx incompris;
J'unis un cœur de neige à la blancheur des cygnes;
Je hais le mouvement qui déplace les lignes,
Et jamais je ne pleure et jamais je ne ris.

Les poètes, devant mes grandes attitudes,
Que j'ai l'air d'emprunter aux plus fiers monuments,
Consumeront leurs jours en d'austères études;

Car j'ai, pour fasciner ces dociles amants,
De purs miroirs qui font toutes choses plus belles:
Mes yeux, mes larges yeux aux clartés éternelles!

....

Beauty

I am fair, o mortals, as a dream of stone, and my bosom, on which each man has bruised himself in turn, is made to inspire in the poet a love eternal and dumb as matter.

I reign in the azure heights like a sphinx whom no one understands; I combine a heart of snow with the whiteness of swans; I hate movement which disturbs lines, and never do I weep and never do I laugh.

Poets, faced by my grand poses, which I seem to have borrowed from the proudest monuments, will use up their days in austere studies;

For I have something to keep those docile lovers enthralled: pure mirrors which make all things more beautiful, my eyes, my wide eyes with their eternal brightness.

10 (XVIII) L'Idéal

Ce ne seront jamais ces beautés de vignettes,
Produits avariés, nés d'un siècle vaurien,
Ces pieds à brodequins, ces doigts à castagnettes,
Qui sauront satisfaire un cœur comme le mien.

Je laisse à Gavarni, poète des chloroses,
Son troupeau gazouillant de beautés d'hôpital,
Car je ne puis trouver parmi ces pâles roses
Une fleur qui ressemble à mon rouge idéal.

Ce qu'il faut à ce cœur profond comme un abîme,
C'est vous, Lady Macbeth, âme puissante au crime,
Rêve d'Eschyle éclos au climat des autans;

Ou bien toi, grande Nuit, fille de Michel-Ange,
Qui tors paisiblement dans une pose étrange
Tes appas façonnés aux bouches des Titans!

....

The Ideal

It will take more than those picture-paper beauties, spoiled products, born of
a worthless century, those feet in tight boots, those fingers made for
castanets, to satisfy a heart like mine.

Gavarni, the poet of anaemia, can keep his twittering flock of hospital
beauties, for I shall never find among those pallid roses a flower which
resembles my red ideal.

What this heart, deep as an abyss, needs is you, Lady Macbeth, soul full of
power for crime, dream of Aeschylus hatched out in the country of gales;

Or you, great Night, daughter of Michelangelo, peacefully twisting in a
strange posture your charms shaped for the mouths of Titans.

11 (XIX) La Géante

Du temps que la Nature en sa verve puissante
Concevait chaque jour des enfants monstrueux,
J'eusse aimé vivre auprès d'une jeune géante,
Comme aux pieds d'une reine un chat voluptueux.

J'eusse aimé voir son corps fleurir avec son âme
Et grandir librement dans ses terribles jeux;
Deviner si son cœur couve une sombre flamme
Aux humides brouillards qui nagent dans ses yeux;

Parcourir à loisir ses magnifiques formes;
Ramper sur le versant de ses genoux énormes,
Et parfois en été, quand les soleils malsains,

Lasse, la font s'étendre à travers la campagne,
Dormir nonchalamment à l'ombre de ses seins,
Comme un hameau paisible au pied d'une montagne.

....

The Giantess

In the days when Nature, in her playful power, conceived every day some new, monstrous children, I should have liked to live with a young giantess, like a voluptuous cat at the feet of a queen.

I should have liked to see her body flower along with her soul, and grow freely in her terrifying games; to guess whether her soul is harbouring some dark flame by the damp mists hanging in her eyes;

To walk at my ease over her magnificent form; to crawl up the slope of her huge knees; and sometimes in summer, when the unhealthy suns

Tire her and make her lie down across the countryside, to sleep carelessly in the shadow of her breasts, like a peaceful hamlet at the foot of a mountain.

12 (XXI) Hymne à la Beauté

Viens-tu du ciel profond ou sors-tu de l'abîme,
O Beauté? ton regard, infernal et divin,
Verse confusément le bienfait et le crime,
Et l'on peut pour cela te comparer au vin.

Tu contiens dans ton œil le couchant et l'aurore;
Tu répands des parfums comme un soir orageux;
Tes baisers sont un philtre et ta bouche une amphore
Qui font le héros lâche et l'enfant courageux.

Sors-tu du gouffre noir ou descends-tu des astres?
Le Destin charmé suit tes jupons comme un chien;
Tu sèmes au hasard la joie et les désastres,
Et tu gouvernes tout et ne réponds de rien.

Tu marches sur des morts, Beauté, dont tu te moques;
De tes bijoux l'Horreur n'est pas le moins charmant,
Et le Meurtre, parmi tes plus chères breloques,
Sur ton ventre orgueilleux danse amoureusement.

....

Hymn to Beauty

Do you come from the depths of heaven or up from the pit, o Beauty? The look of your eyes, hellish and divine, pours out indiscriminately blessings and crime, and that is why you can be compared to wine.

You hold in your eyes sunset and dawn; you exude perfumes like a stormy evening; your kisses are a philtre and your mouth an amphora that make the hero cowardly and the boy courageous.

Do you come from the black gulf or down from the stars? Destiny, spellbound, follows your petticoats like a dog; you sow at random joy and disasters, and you rule everything and answer for nothing.

You walk over dead men, Beauty, for whom you care nothing; of your jewels Horror is not least charming, and Murder, among your dearest trinkets, there on your proud belly dances amorously.

L'éphémère ébloui vole vers toi, chandelle,
Crépite, flambe et dit: Bénissons ce flambeau!
L'amoureux pantelant incliné sur sa belle
A l'air d'un moribond caressant son tombeau.

Que tu viennes du ciel ou de l'enfer, qu'importe,
O Beauté! monstre énorme, effrayant, ingénu!
Si ton œil, ton souris, ton pied, m'ouvrent la porte
D'un Infini que j'aime et n'ai jamais connu?

De Satan ou de Dieu, qu'importe? Ange ou Sirène,
Qu'importe, si tu rends, – fée aux yeux de velours,
Rythme, parfum, lueur, ô mon unique reine! –
L'univers moins hideux et les instants moins lourds?

....

The dazzled moth flies towards you, the candle, crackles, flares up and
says 'Let us bless this light.' The panting lover bent over his fair one looks
like a dying man caressing his tomb.

Let it be heaven or hell you come from, what do I care, o Beauty, huge,
terrifying, innocent monster, if your eye, your smile, your foot can open the
door for me to an Infinite that I love and that I have never known.

From Satan or from God, what does it matter? Angel or Siren, what
matter, if – velvet-eyed fairy, rhythm, perfume, gleaming, o my only queen
– you make the universe less hideous and the passing seconds less heavy?

13 (XXIII) La Chevelure

O toison, moutonnant jusque sur l'encolure!
O boucles! O parfum chargé de nonchaloir!
Extase! Pour peupler ce soir l'alcôve obscure
Des souvenirs dormant dans cette chevelure,
Je la veux agiter dans l'air comme un mouchoir!

La langoureuse Asie et la brûlante Afrique,
Toute un monde lointain, absent, presque défunt,
Vit dans tes profondeurs, forêt aromatique!
Comme d'autres esprits voguent sur la musique,
Le mien, ô mon amour! nage sur ton parfum.

J'irai là-bas où l'arbre et l'homme, pleins de sève,
Se pâment longuement sous l'ardeur des climats;
Fortes tresses, soyez la houle qui m'enlève!
Tu contiens, mer d'ébène, un éblouissant rêve
De voiles, de rameurs, de flammes et de mâts:

....

The Head of Hair

O fleece, tumbling in waves upon the neck! o curls! o perfume heavy with carelessness! Ecstasy! To fill, this evening, the dark alcove with the memories sleeping in this head of hair, I want to wave it in the air like a handkerchief.

Languorous Asia and burning Africa, a whole world, distant, absent, which has almost ceased to be, lives in your depths, scented forest! As other minds float on music, mine, o my love, swims on your perfume.

I will go far away where trees and men, full of sap, swoon in long ecstasies under the heat of the suns; strong tresses, be the sea that bears me away! You hold within you, ebony sea, a dazzling dream of sails, of rowers, of flames and of masts:

Un port retentissant où mon âme peut boire
A grands flots le parfum, le son et la couleur;
Où les vaisseaux, glissant dans l'or et dans la moire,
Ouvrent leurs vastes bras pour embrasser la gloire
D'un ciel pur où frémit l'éternelle chaleur.

Je plongerai ma tête amoureuse d'ivresse
Dans ce noir océan où l'autre est enfermé;
Et mon esprit subtil que le roulis caresse
Saura vous retrouver, ô féconde paresse,
Infinis bercements du loisir embaumé!

Cheveux bleus, pavillon de ténèbres tendues,
Vous me rendez l'azur du ciel immense et rond;
Sur les bords duvetés de vos mèches tordues
Je m'enivre ardemment des senteurs confondues
De l'huile de coco, du musc et du goudron.

Longtemps! toujours! ma main dans ta crinière lourde
Sèmera le rubis, la perle et le saphir,
Afin qu'à mon désir tu ne sois jàmais sourde!
N'es–tu pas l'oasis où je rêve, et la gourde
Où je hume à longs traits le vin du souvenir?

....

An echoing port where my soul can drink great draughts of perfume,
sound and colour; where the ships, sliding amid gold and silk, open their
vast arms to embrace the glory of a pure sky trembling with eternal heat.

I will plunge my head, loving, enraptured, into this dark ocean where the
other is enclosed; and my subtle spirit, caressed by the rolling of the waves,
will find you once more, o fruitful idleness, infinite rockings of perfumed
leisure.

Blue hair, enclosing tent of darkness, you bring back to me the blue of the
measureless round sky; on the fluffy edges of your twisted locks I greedily
breathe in the intoxicating, mixed smell of coconut oil, musk and tar.

For a long time, for ever, my hand, in your heavy mane, will sow rubies,
pearls and sapphires, so that my desire may never find you deaf. Are you not
the oasis where I dream, and the gourd from which I drink in long draughts
the wine of memory?

14 (XXIV)

Je t'adore à l'égal de la voûte nocturne,
O vase de tristesse, ô grande taciturne,
Et t'aime d'autant plus, belle, que tu me fuis,
Et que tu me parais, ornement de mes nuits,
Plus ironiquement accumuler les lieues
Qui séparent mes bras des immensités bleues.

Je m'avance à l'attaque, et je grimpe aux assauts,
Comme après un cadavre un chœur de vermisseaux,
Et je chéris, ô bête implacable et cruelle!
Jusqu'à cette froideur par où tu m'es plus belle!

....

14

I worship you as I worship the vault of the night sky, o vessel of sadness, o great silent one, and love you the more, fair one, the more you flee me, and seem, ornament of my nights, the more ironically to multiply the leagues that separate my arms from the blue immensities.

I move to the attack, and climb into position, like a choir of maggots assaulting a corpse, and I cherish, o implacable and cruel animal, that very coldness which makes you more beautiful to me.

15 (XXV)

Tu mettrais l'univers entier dans ta ruelle,
Femme impure! L'ennui rend ton âme cruelle.
Pour exercer tes dents à ce jeu singulier,
Il te faut chaque jour un cœur au râtelier.
Tes yeux, illuminés ainsi que des boutiques
Et des ifs flamboyants dans les fêtes publiques,
Usent insolemment d'un pouvoir emprunté,
Sans connaître jamais la loi de leur beauté.

Machine aveugle et sourde, en cruautés féconde!
Salutaire instrument, buveur du sang du monde,
Comment n'as-tu pas honte et comment n'as-tu pas
Devant tous les miroirs vu pâlir tes appas?
La grandeur de ce mal où tu te crois savante
Ne t'a donc jamais fait reculer d'épouvante,
Quand la nature, grande en ses desseins cachés,
De toi se sert, ô femme, ô reine des péchés,
— De toi, vil animal, — pour pétrir un génie?

O fangeuse grandeur! sublime ignominie!

....

15

You would have the whole universe waiting by your bed, impure woman! Boredom makes your soul cruel. To exercise your teeth in that singular game, you need a new heart in the manger every day. Your eyes, lit up like shops or illuminated yew trees at public festivals, insolently make use of a borrowed power, without ever knowing the law of their beauty.

    Blind and deaf machine, fertile in cruelties! Saving instrument, drinker of the world's blood, how can you not be ashamed, and how can you not have seen in every mirror the fading of your charms? The greatness of this evil in which you consider yourself knowledgeable, has it never, then, made you draw back in fear, when Nature, great in her hidden designs, makes use of you, o woman, o queen of sin — of you, base animal — to mould a genius?

    O sullied grandeur! sublime ignominy!

16 (xxvi) Sed Non Satiata

Bizarre déité, brune comme les nuits,
Au parfum-mélangé de musc et de havane,
Œuvre de quelque obi, le Faust de la savane,
Sorcière au flanc d'ébène, enfant des noirs minuits,

Je préfère au constance, à l'opium, au nuits,
L'élixir de ta bouche où l'amour se pavane;
Quand vers toi mes désirs partent en caravane,
Tes yeux sont la citerne où boivent mes ennuis.

Par ces deux grands yeux noirs, soupiraux de ton âme,
O démon sans pitié! verse-moi moins de flamme;
Je ne suis pas le Styx pour t'embrasser neuf fois,

Hélas! et je ne puis, Mégère libertine,
Pour briser ton courage et te mettre aux abois,
Dans l'enfer de ton lit devenir Proserpine!

....

Sed Non Satiata

Bizarre deity, dark as nights, with your mixed perfume of musk and cigar tobacco, work of some witch-doctor, the Faust of the savanna, ebony-flanked witch, child of dark midnights,

I prefer to Cape wine, to opium, to burgundy, the elixir of your mouth where love parades itself; when the caravan of my desires sets out towards you, your eyes are the cistern where my troubles drink.

Through those two great black eyes, smokeholes of your soul, o pitiless demon, pour out less flame upon me; I am not the Styx to embrace you nine times, alas!

And I cannot, o libertine Megaera, break your spirit and make you beg for mercy by, in the hell of your bed, becoming Proserpina.

17 (XXVII)

Avec ses vêtements ondoyants et nacrés,
Même quand elle marche on croirait qu'elle danse,
Comme ces longs serpents que les jongleurs sacrés
Au bout de leurs bâtons agitent en cadence.

Comme le sable morne et l'azur des déserts,
Insensibles tous deux à l'humaine souffrance,
Comme les longs réseaux de la houle des mers,
Elle se développe avec indifférence.

Ses yeux polis sont faits de minéraux charmants,
Et dans cette nature étrange et symbolique
Où l'ange inviolé se mêle au sphinx antique,

Où tout n'est qu'or, acier, lumière et diamants,
Resplendit à jamais, comme un astre inutile,
La froide majesté de la femme stérile.

....

17

With her undulating, iridescent clothes, even when she walks you would think she is dancing, like those long snakes that sacred jugglers shake rhythmically on the ends of their sticks.

Like the bleak sand and the blue sky of deserts, equally unmoved by human suffering; like the long wave-patterns of the seas, she unfolds in her indifference.

Her polished eyes are made of charming minerals, and in this strange and symbolic nature where the inviolate angel mingles with the ancient sphinx,

Where everything is made of gold, steel, light and diamonds, there shines forth for ever, like a useless star, the cold majesty of the sterile woman.

18 (XXVIII) Le Serpent qui Danse

Que j'aime voir, chère indolente,
    De ton corps si beau,
Comme une étoffe vacillante,
    Miroiter la peau!

Sur ta chevelure profonde
    Aux âcres parfums,
Mer odorante et vagabonde
    Aux flots bleus et bruns,

Comme un navire qui s'éveille
    Au vent du matin,
Mon âme rêveuse appareille
    Pour un ciel lointain.

Tes yeux, où rien ne se révèle
    De doux ni d'amer,
Sont deux bijoux froids où se mêle
    L'or avec le fer.

....

The Dancing Serpent

How I love to look, dear indolent one, at your beautiful body and see, like a shot silk, the changing gleam of your skin!

    On your deep hair, with its bitter perfumes, a scented and wandering sea of blue and brown waves,

    Like a ship stirring with the wind of morning my dreamy soul sets sail for a distant sky.

    Your eyes, in which nothing is revealed, sweet or bitter, are two cold jewels in which gold mingles with iron.

A te voir marcher en cadence,
　　Belle d'abandon,
On dirait un serpent qui danse
　　Au bout d'un bâton.

Sous le fardeau de ta paresse
　　Ta tête d'enfant
Se balance avec la mollesse
　　D'un jeune éléphant,

Et ton corps se penche et s'allonge
　　Comme un fin vaisseau
Qui roule bord sur bord et plonge
　　Ses vergues dans l'eau.

Comme un flot grossi par la fonte
　　Des glaciers grondants,
Quand l'eau de ta bouche remonte
　　Au bord de tes dents,

Je crois boire un vin de Bohême,
　　Amer et vainqueur,
Un ciel liquide qui parsème
　　D'étoiles mon cœur!

....

Seeing your rhythmic walk, beautiful in its abandon, one thinks of a
serpent dancing at the end of a stick.

Under the weight of your laziness, your child's head hangs with the soft
looseness of a young elephant's.

And your body sways and stretches like an elegant ship rolling from side
to side and pitching its yards in the water.

Like a stream swollen by the melting of grinding glaciers, when the water
of your mouth rises to the edge of your teeth,

I feel I am drinking a Bohemian wine, bitter and overpowering, a liquid
sky which scatters my heart with stars.

19 (XXIX) Une Charogne

Rappelez-vous l'objet que nous vîmes, mon âme,
    Ce beau matin d'été si doux:
Au détour d'un sentier une charogne infâme
    Sur un lit semé de cailloux,

Les jambes en l'air, comme une femme lubrique,
    Brûlante et suant les poisons,
Ouvrait d'une façon nonchalante et cynique
    Son ventre plein d'exhalaisons.

Le soleil rayonnait sur cette pourriture,
    Comme afin de la cuire à point,
Et de rendre au centuple à la grande Nature
    Tout ce qu'ensemble elle avait joint;

Et le ciel regardait la carcasse superbe
    Comme une fleur s'épanouir.
La puanteur était si forte, que sur l'herbe
    Vous crûtes vous évanouir.

....

A Carcass

Remember the sight we saw, my soul, that fine, mild summer morning:
round a turning in the path a disgusting carcass on a bed scattered with
stones,

    Its legs in the air like a woman on heat, burning and sweating poisons,
was displaying, in casual and shameless fashion, its belly, full of noxious
vapours.

    The sun was shining on that mass of rottenness as if to cook it to
perfection, and to give back a hundredfold to great Nature all that she had
joined together;

    And heaven watched the splendid carcass unfolding like a flower. The
stench was so strong that you thought you would faint right there, on the
grass.

Les mouches bourdonnaient sur ce ventre putride,
  D'où sortaient de noirs bataillons
De larves, qui coulaient comme un épais liquide
  Le long de ces vivants haillons.

Tout cela descendait, montait comme une vague,
  Ou s'élançait en pétillant;
On eût dit que le corps, enflé d'un souffle vague,
  Vivait en se multipliant.

Et ce monde rendait une étrange musique,
  Comme l'eau courante et le vent,
Ou le grain qu'un vanneur d'un mouvement rythmique
  Agite et tourne dans son van.

Les formes s'effaçaient et n'étaient plus qu'un rêve,
  Une ébauche lente à venir,
Sur la toile oubliée, et que l'artiste achève
  Seulement par le souvenir.

Derrière les rochers une chienne inquiète
  Nous regardait d'un œil fâché,
Epiant le moment de reprendre au squelette
  Le morceau qu'elle avait lâché.

....

The flies were buzzing on that putrid belly, from which issued black battalions of larvae, flowing like a thick liquid along those living rags.

The whole mass fell and rose like a wave, or erupted in sparkling foam; you would have said that the body, filled with some mysterious breath, was living and multiplying.

And this world was emitting a strange music, like running water and wind, or the grain which a winnower with a rhythmic movement shakes and turns in his winnowing-basket.

The shapes were fading and were now only a dream, a sketch slow to take shape on the forgotten canvas, which the artist completes only in his memory.

Behind the rocks a restless bitch was watching us with angry eyes, waiting for the moment to reclaim from the skeleton the titbit she had left behind.

– Et pourtant vous serez semblable à cette ordure,
    A cette horrible infection,
Etoile de mes yeux, soleil de ma nature,
    Vous, mon ange et ma passion!

Oui! telle vous serez, ô la reine des grâces,
    Après les derniers sacrements,
Quand vous irez, sous l'herbe et les floraisons grasses,
    Moisir parmi les ossements.

Alors, ô ma beauté! dites à la vermine
    Qui vous mangera de baisers,
Que j'ai gardé la forme et l'essence divine
    De mes amours décomposés!

20 (xxx) De Profundis Clamavi

J'implore ta pitié, Toi, l'unique que j'aime,
Du fond du gouffre obscur où mon cœur est tombé.
C'est un univers morne à l'horizon plombé,
Où nagent dans la nuit l'horreur et le blasphème;

....

And yet you will be like that ordure, that horrible, unclean thing, o star of my eyes, sun of my nature, you, my angel and my passion!

Yes, such you will be, o queen of grace, after the last sacraments, when you will go, under the grass and the fat flowering weeds, to moulder among the dead bones.

Then, o my beauty, say to the vermin who will devour you with kisses, that I have kept the form and the divine essence of my decomposed loves.

De Profundis Clamavi

I implore your pity, you, the sole being that I love, from the depths of the dark pit where my heart has fallen. It is a bleak universe with leaden horizons in whose darkness float horror and blasphemy;

Un soleil sans chaleur plane au-dessus six mois,
Et les six autres mois la nuit couvre la terre;
C'est un pays plus nu que la terre polaire;
— Ni bêtes, ni ruisseaux, ni verdure, ni bois!

Or il n'est pas d'horreur au monde qui surpasse
La froide cruauté de ce soleil de glace
Et cette immense nuit semblable au vieux Chaos;

Je jalouse le sort des plus vils animaux
Qui peuvent se plonger dans un sommeil stupide,
Tant l'écheveau du temps lentement se dévide!

21 (XXXI) Le Vampire

Toi qui, comme un coup de couteau,
Dans mon cœur plaintif es entrée;
Toi qui, forte comme un troupeau
De démons, vins, folle et parée,

....

A sun without heat hangs above it for six months and for the other six
months night covers the earth. It is a country barer than the lands at the pole
— no animals, no streams, no green growth, no woods!

Now there is no horror in the world that can surpass the cold cruelty of
that icy sun, and that vast night, boundless as old Chaos;

I envy the fate of the lowest animals who can plunge into a stupor of
sleep, so slowly does the spool of time unwind.

The Vampire

You who, like a knife thrust, entered my cringing heart; you who, strong as
a troop of demons, came, gaily adorned,

De mon esprit humilié
Faire ton lit et ton domaine;
— Infâme à qui je suis lié
Comme le forçat à la chaîne,

Comme au jeu le joueur têtu,
Comme à la bouteille l'ivrogne,
Comme aux vermines la charogne,
— Maudite, maudite sois-tu!

J'ai prié le glaive rapide
De conquérir ma liberté,
Et j'ai dit au poison perfide
De secourir ma lâcheté.

Hélas! le poison et le glaive
M'ont pris en dédain et m'ont dit:
«Tu n'es pas digne qu'on t'enlève
A ton esclavage maudit,

Imbécile! — de son empire
Si nos efforts te délivraient,
Tes baisers ressusciteraient
Le cadavre de ton vampire!»

....

To my prostrate spirit, to make of it your bed and your kingdom;
Wretch to whom I am bound as the convict to his chain,

As the stubborn gambler to the table, as the drunkard to the bottle, as the
corpse to the worms — curses, curses be upon you!

I begged the rapid blade to win me my liberty, and I called on treacherous
poison to help out my cowardice.

Alas! poison and sword turned from me and said, 'You are not worthy to
be taken from your accursed slavery,

'Fool! — if from her power our efforts were to deliver you, your kisses
would resuscitate the body of your vampire!'

22 (XXXIV) Le Chat

Viens, mon beau chat, sur mon cœur amoureux;
    Retiens les griffes de ta patte,
Et laisse-moi plonger dans tes beaux yeux,
    Mêlés de métal et d'agate.

Lorsque mes doigts caressent à loisir
    Ta tête et ton dos élastique,
Et que ma main s'enivre du plaisir
    De palper ton corps électrique,

Je vois ma femme en esprit. Son regard,
    Comme le tien, aimable bête,
Profond et froid, coupe et fend comme un dard,

    Et, des pieds jusques à la tête,
Un air subtil, un dangereux parfum
    Nagent autour de son corps brun.

....

The Cat

Come, my dear cat, here on my lovesick heart; hold in your claws, and let me plunge into your beautiful eyes with their mixture of metal and agate.

When my fingers are slowly stroking your head and your supple back, and my hand is becoming intoxicated with the pleasure of touching your electric body,

I see my woman in my mind's eye. Her look, like yours, delightful creature, is deep and cold, and cuts and splits like a blade,

And, from her feet to her head, a subtle air, a dangerous perfume float around her brown body.

23 (XXXVI) Le Balcon

Mère des souvenirs, maîtresse des maîtresses,
O toi, tous mes plaisirs! ô toi, tous mes devoirs!
Tu te rappelleras la beauté des caresses,
La douceur du foyer et le charme des soirs,
Mère des souvenirs, maîtresse des maîtresses!

Les soirs illuminés par l'ardeur du charbon,
Et les soirs au balcon, voilés de vapeurs roses.
Que ton sein m'était doux! que ton cœur m'était bon!
Nous avons dit souvent d'impérissables choses
Les soirs illuminés par l'ardeur du charbon.

Que les soleils sont beaux dans les chaudes soirées!
Que l'espace est profond! que le cœur est puissant!
En me penchant vers toi, reine des adorées,
Je croyais respirer le parfum de ton sang.
Que les soleils sont beaux dans les chaudes soirées!

....

The Balcony

Mother of memories, mistress of mistresses, o you, all my pleasures! o you, all my duties! You will remember the beauty of caresses, the sweet warmth of the fireside and the charm of evenings, mother of memories, mistress of mistresses!

The evenings lit up by the burning of coals and the evenings on the balcony, veiled in pink vapours. How sweet your breast was to me, how warm your heart! We often said unforgettable things on those evenings lit up by the burning of coals.

How beautiful the suns are in warm evenings! How deep space is, how powerful the heart! As I leaned towards you, queen of adored ones, I felt I was breathing in the perfume of your blood. How beautiful the suns are in warm evenings!

La nuit s'épaississait ainsi qu'une cloison,
Et mes yeux dans le noir devinaient tes prunelles,
Et je buvais ton souffle, ô douceur! ô poison!
Et tes pieds s'endormaient dans mes mains fraternelles.
La nuit s'épaississait ainsi qu'une cloison.

Je sais l'art d'évoquer les minutes heureuses,
Et revis mon passé blotti dans tes genoux.
Car à quoi bon chercher tes beautés langoureuses
Ailleurs qu'en ton cher corps et qu'en ton cœur si doux?
Je sais l'art d'évoquer les minutes heureuses!

Ces serments, ces parfums, ces baisers infinis,
Renaîtront-ils d'un gouffre interdit à nos sondes,
Comme montent au ciel les soleils rajeunis
Après s'être lavés au fond des mers profondes?
– O serments! ô parfums! ô baisers infinis!

....

Night thickened like a wall and my eyes, in the darkness, guessed at your pupils, and I drank in your breath, o sweetness! o poison! And your feet drifted into sleep, held in my brotherly hands. Night thickened like a wall.

I know the art of calling up moments of happiness and relive my past, my head buried in your lap. For why would I look for your languorous beauties elsewhere than in your dear body and in your loving heart? I know the art of calling up moments of happiness.

Those promises, those perfumes, those endless kisses, will they be born again from deeps our plumb-lines cannot reach, as the rejuvenated suns rise up to heaven, having washed themselves in the depths of the seas? O promises, perfumes, endless kisses!

24 (XXXVII) Le Possédé

Le soleil s'est couvert d'un crêpe. Comme lui,
O Lune de ma vie! emmitoufle-toi d'ombre;
Dors ou fume à ton gré; sois muette, sois sombre,
Et plonge tout entière au gouffre de l'Ennui;

Je t'aime ainsi! Pourtant, si tu veux aujourd'hui,
Comme un astre éclipsé qui sort de la pénombre,
Te pavaner aux lieux que la Folie encombre,
C'est bien! Charmant poignard, jailli de ton étui!

Allume ta prunelle à la flamme des lustres!
Allume le désir dans les regards des rustres!
Tout de toi m'est plaisir, morbide ou pétulant;

Sois ce que tu voudras, nuit noire, rouge aurore;
Il n'est pas une fibre en tout mon corps tremblant
Qui ne crie: *O mon cher Belzébuth, je t'adore!*

....

The Possessed One

The sun has covered himself with a mourning veil. Like him, o Moon of my
life, muffle yourself up in shadow; sleep or smoke as you please, be mute, be
sombre, and plunge yourself wholly into the gulf of Tedium.

  I like you that way! On the other hand, if you wish, today, like an
eclipsed star coming out of its penumbra, to parade in the places where Folly
crowds, that's good too. Charming dagger, spring from your scabbard!

  Light up your eyes at the flame of the chandeliers! Light up desire in the
eyes of country clods! Everything that comes from you is pleasure to me,
sickly or vivacious;

  Be what you will, black night, red dawn; there is not a fibre in my whole,
trembling body but cries out, 'O my dear Beelzebub, I adore you!'

25 (XXXVIII) Un Fantôme

I LES TÉNÈBRES

Dans les caveaux d'insondable tristesse
Où le Destin m'a déjà relégué;
Où jamais n'entre un rayon rose et gai;
Où, seul avec la Nuit, maussade hôtesse,

Je suis comme un peintre qu'un Dieu moqueur
Condamne à peindre, hélas! sur les ténèbres;
Où, cuisinier aux appétits funèbres,
Je fais bouillir et je mange mon cœur,

Par instants brille, et s'allonge, et s'étale
Un spectre fait de grâce et de splendeur.
A sa rêveuse allure orientale,

Quand il atteint sa totale grandeur,
Je reconnais ma belle visiteuse:
C'est Elle! noire et pourtant lumineuse.

....

A Ghost

I THE DARKNESS

In the vaults of fathomless sadness to which Destiny has already banished me; where no pink, gay ray of light ever enters; where, alone with Night, a gloomy landlady,

I am like a painter condemned by a mocking God to paint, alas, upon the darkness; where, a cook with deathly appetites, I constantly boil and eat my own heart;

There sometimes shines forth, and stretches, and displays itself, a spectre made of grace and splendour. By its dreamy, oriental movements,

When it reaches its full stature, I recognize my beautiful visitor: it is She, black and yet luminous!

II LE PARFUM

Lecteur, as-tu quelquefois respiré
Avec ivresse et lente gourmandise
Ce grain d'encens qui remplit une église,
Ou d'un sachet le musc invétéré?

Charme profond, magique, dont nous grise
Dans le présent le passé restauré!
Ainsi l'amant sur un corps adoré
Du souvenir cueille la fleur exquise.

De ses cheveux élastiques et lourds,
Vivant sachet, encensoir de l'alcôve,
Une senteur montait, sauvage et fauve,

Et des habits, mousseline ou velours,
Tout imprégnés de sa jeunesse pure,
Se dégageait un parfum de fourrure.

....

II THE PERFUME

Reader, have you sometimes breathed in, with intoxication and slow greediness, the grain of incense which fills a church or the persistent musk of a sachet?

Profound, magical spell which captures us when, in the present, the past is restored! Even so the lover from an adored body plucks memory's exquisite flower.

From her elastic, heavy hair, a living sachet, thurible of the alcove, a smell arose, savage and wild,

And from the clothes, muslin or velvet, all impregnated with her pure youthfulness, there emanated a scent of fur.

III LE CADRE

Comme un beau cadre ajoute à la peinture,
Bien qu'elle soit d'un pinceau très vanté,
Je ne sais quoi d'étrange et d'enchanté
En l'isolant de l'immense nature,

Ainsi bijoux, meubles, métaux, dorure,
S'adaptaient juste à sa rare beauté;
Rien n'offusquait sa parfaite clarté,
Et tout semblait lui servir de bordure.

Même on eût dit parfois qu'elle croyait
Que tout voulait l'aimer; elle noyait
Sa nudité voluptueusement

Dans les baisers du satin et du linge,
Et lente ou brusque, à chaque mouvement
Montrait la grâce enfantine du singe.

....

III THE FRAME

As a fine frame adds to the picture, even if it is by a very famous hand,
something strange and enchanted, isolating it from the immensity of nature,

So jewels, furniture, metals, gilding, fitted themselves exactly around her
rare beauty; nothing obscured her perfect brightness and everything seemed
to act as a border around her.

You would even sometimes have said that she believed everything wanted
to make love to her; she drowned her nakedness voluptuously

In the kisses of satin and of linen and, slowly or abruptly, showed in each
movement the childish grace of the monkey.

IV LE PORTRAIT

La Maladie et la Mort font des cendres
De tout le feu qui pour nous flamboya.
De ces grands yeux si fervents et si tendres,
De cette bouche où mon cœur se noya,

De ces baisers puissants comme un dictame,
De ces transports plus vifs que des rayons,
Que reste-t-il? C'est affreux, ô mon âme!
Rien qu'un dessin fort pâle, aux trois crayons,

Qui, comme moi, meurt dans la solitude,
Et que le Temps, injurieux vieillard,
Chaque jour frotte avec son aile rude . . .

Noir assassin de la Vie et de l'Art,
Tu ne tueras jamais dans ma mémoire
Celle qui fut mon plaisir et ma gloire!

....

IV THE PORTRAIT

Sickness and Death turn to ashes all the fire that blazed for us. Of those great eyes, so fervent and so tender, of that mouth where my heart drowned,

Of those kisses powerful as a wound-salve, of those transports more intense than the sun's rays, what is there left? It is terrible, o my soul! Nothing but a drawing, very pale, in three colours of chalk,

Which, like me, is dying in solitude, and which Time, that offensive old man, rubs every day with his harsh wing . . .

Black assassin of Life and Art, you will never kill in my memory her who was my pleasure and my glory.

26 (XXXIX)

Je te donne ces vers afin que si mon nom
Aborde heureusement aux époques lointaines,
Et fait rêver un soir les cervelles humaines,
Vaisseau favorisé par un grand aquilon,

Ta mémoire, pareille aux fables incertaines,
Fatigue le lecteur ainsi qu'un tympanon,
Et par un fraternel et mystique chaînon
Reste comme pendue à mes rimes hautaines;

Etre maudit à qui, de l'abîme profond
Jusqu'au plus haut du ciel, rien, hors moi, ne répond!
— O toi qui, comme une ombre à la trace éphémère,

Foules d'un pied léger et d'un regard serein
Les stupides mortels qui t'ont jugée amère,
Statue aux yeux de jais, grand ange au front d'airain!

....

26

I give you these lines so that if my name makes a happy landfall in distant epochs and, one evening, sets human brains dreaming, a ship driven on by a great north wind,

The memory of you, like uncertain fables, may tire the reader like a rhythmic drone and, by the link of a brotherly and mystical chain, remain attached, as it were, to my lofty rhymes.

Accursed being to whom, from the depths of the abyss to the highest heaven, nothing, apart from myself, corresponds! — O you, who like a shadow with fleeting step,

Tread underfoot, lightly and with a serene gaze, the stupid mortals who called you bitter, statue with eyes of jet, great angel with your forehead of bronze.

27 (XLI) Tout Entière

Le Démon, dans ma chambre haute,
Ce matin est venu me voir,
Et, tâchant à me prendre en faute,
Me dit: «Je voudrais bien savoir,

Parmi toutes les belles choses
Dont est fait son enchantement,
Parmi les objets noirs ou roses
Qui composent son corps charmant,

Quel est le plus doux.» – O mon âme!
Tu répondis à l'Abhorré:
«Puisqu'en Elle tout est dictame,
Rien ne peut être préféré.

Lorsque tout me ravit, j'ignore
Si quelque chose me séduit.
Elle éblouit comme l'Aurore
Et console comme la Nuit;

....

All of Her

The Devil, in my high chamber, came this morning to see me, and, trying to catch me out, said, 'I should dearly like to know,

'Among all the beautiful things of which her enchantment is made, among the black or pink objects which make up her charming body

Which is the sweetest?' – O my soul! You replied to the Abhorred One: 'Since in Her everything is balm, nothing can be preferred.

'When everything ravishes me, I do not know if any single thing delights me. She dazzles like the Dawn and consoles like Night;

Et l'harmonie est trop exquise,
Qui gouverne tout son beau corps,
Pour que l'impuissante analyse
En note les nombreux accords.

O métamorphose mystique
De tous mes sens fondus en un!
Son haleine fait la musique,
Comme sa voix fait le parfum!»

28 (XLII)

Que diras-tu ce soir, pauvre âme solitaire,
Que diras-tu, mon cœur, cœur autrefois flétri,
A la très belle, à la très bonne, à la très chère,
Dont le regard divin t'a soudain refleuri?

– Nous mettrons notre orgueil à chanter ses louanges:
Rien ne vaut la douceur de son autorité;
Sa chair spirituelle a le parfum des Anges,
Et son œil nous revêt d'un habit de clarté.

....

'And too exquisite a harmony governs her beautiful body for impotent analysis to be able to note its multiple chords.

'O mystic metamorphosis of all my senses melted into one! Her breath makes the music as her voice makes the perfume.'

28

What will you say this evening, poor solitary soul, what will you say, my heart, once-withered heart, to the most beautiful, the best, the dearest one, whose divine look has suddenly made you flower again?

We shall set our pride in singing her praises. Nothing equals the sweetness of her authority; her spiritual flesh has the scent of Angels, and her eye clothes us in a garment of light.

Que ce soit dans la nuit et dans la solitude,
Que ce soit dans la rue et dans la multitude,
Son fantôme dans l'air danse comme un flambeau.

Parfois il parle et dit: «Je suis belle, et j'ordonne
Que pour l'amour de moi vous n'aimiez que le Beau;
Je suis l'Ange gardien, la Muse et la Madone.»

29 (XLIII) Le Flambeau Vivant

Ils marchent devant moi, ces Yeux pleins de lumières,
Qu'un Ange très savant a sans doute aimantés;
Ils marchent, ces divins frères qui sont mes frères,
Secouant dans mes yeux leurs feux diamantés.

Me sauvant de tout piège et de tout péché grave,
Ils conduisent mes pas dans la route du Beau;
Ils sont mes serviteurs et je suis leur esclave;
Tout mon être obéit à ce vivant flambeau.

....

Be it in the night and in solitude, be it in the street and in the multitude, her phantom dances in the air like a burning brand.

Sometimes it speaks and says: 'I am beautiful, and I command that for love of me you love only the Beautiful; I am the guardian Angel, the Muse and the Madonna!'

The Living Torch

They walk before me, those light-filled eyes, which a very wise Angel magnetized, no doubt; they walk, those divine brothers who are my brothers, shaking into my eyes their glittering fires.

Saving me from all snares and all grave sins, they lead my steps in the path of the Beautiful; they are my servants and I am their slave; all my being obeys this living torch.

Charmants Yeux, vous brillez de la clarté mystique
Qu'ont les cierges brûlant en plein jour; le soleil
Rougit, mais n'éteint pas leur flamme fantastique;

Ils célèbrent la Mort, vous chantez le Réveil;
Vous marchez en chantant le réveil de mon âme,
Astres dont nul soleil ne peut flétrir la flamme!

30 (XLIV) Réversibilité

Ange plein de gaieté, connaissez-vous l'angoisse,
La honte, les remords, les sanglots, les ennuis,
Et les vagues terreurs de ces affreuses nuits
Qui compriment le cœur comme un papier qu'on froisse?
Ange plein de gaieté, connaissez-vous l'angoisse?

Ange plein de bonté, connaissez-vous la haine,
Les poings crispés dans l'ombre et les larmes de fiel,
Quand la Vengeance bat son infernal rappel,
Et de nos facultés se fait le capitaine?
Ange plein de bonté, connaissez-vous la haine?

....

Enchanting Eyes, you shine with the mystical brightness of candles
burning in daylight; the sun reddens, but cannot extinguish their eerie flame;
They celebrate Death, you sing of Awakening; you go forth hymning the
awakening of my soul, stars whose flame no sun can wither.

Intercession

Angel full of gaiety, do you know anguish, shame, remorse, tears, sufferings,
and the vague terrors of those dreadful nights that grip the heart as one
crumples a piece of paper? Angel full of gaiety, do you know anguish?
Angel full of goodness, do you know hatred, fists clenched in the shadow
and tears of gall, when Revenge beats its hellish mustering call and makes
itself captain of our faculties? Angel full of goodness, do you know hatred?

Ange plein de santé, connaissez-vous les Fièvres,
Qui, le long des grands murs de l'hospice blafard,
Comme des exilés, s'en vont d'un pied traînard,
Cherchant le soleil rare et remuant les lèvres?
Ange plein de santé, connaissez-vous les Fièvres?

Ange plein de beauté, connaissez-vous les rides,
Et la peur de vieillir, et ce hideux tourment
De lire la secrète horreur du dévouement
Dans des yeux où longtemps burent nos yeux avides?
Ange plein de beauté, connaissez-vous les rides?

Ange plein de bonheur, de joie et de lumières,
David mourant aurait demandé la santé
Aux émanations de ton corps enchanté;
Mais de toi je n'implore, ange, que tes prières,
Ange plein de bonheur, de joie et de lumières!

....

Angel full of health, do you know the Fevers who, along the high walls
of the grey workhouse hospital, like exiles, go dragging their feet, seeking
the elusive sun and muttering to themselves? Angel full of health, do you
know Fevers?

Angel full of beauty, do you know wrinkles, and the fear of growing old,
and the hideous torment of reading the secret horror of fidelity in eyes
where our eyes so long drank greedily? Angel full of beauty, do you know
wrinkles?

Angel full of happiness, of joy and of light, David on his deathbed would
have sought health in the emanations of your enchanted body; but from
you, angel, I beg only your prayers, angel full of happiness, of joy and of
light!

31 (XLV) Confession

Une fois, une seule, aimable et douce femme,
　　A mon bras votre bras poli
S'appuya (sur le fond ténébreux de mon âme
　　Ce souvenir n'est point pâli);

Il était tard; ainsi qu'une médaille neuve
　　La pleine lune s'étalait,
Et la solennité de la nuit, comme un fleuve
　　Sur Paris dormant ruisselait.

Et le long des maisons, sous les portes cochères,
　　Des chats passaient furtivement,
L'oreille au guet, ou bien, comme des ombres chères,
　　Nous accompagnaient lentement.

Tout à coup, au milieu de l'intimité libre
　　Eclose à la pâle clarté,
De vous, riche et sonore instrument où ne vibre
　　Que la radieuse gaieté,

....

Confession

Once, just once, lovable and gentle woman, on my arm your polished arm leaned (on the dark ground of my soul that bright memory has never faded);

It was late; like a new medal the full moon displayed itself, and the solemnity of the night, like a river, streamed over sleeping Paris.

And along the house fronts, under the carriage entrances, cats passed furtively, their ears cocked, or like shades of our dear ones, followed us slowly.

Suddenly, in the middle of the intimate, free mood that had blossomed in the pale light, there came from you, rich and sonorous instrument which resonates only with radiant gaiety,

De vous, claire et joyeuse ainsi qu'une fanfare
    Dans le matin étincelant,
Une note plaintive, une note bizarre
    S'échappa, tout en chancelant

Comme une enfant chétive, horrible, sombre, immonde,
    Dont sa famille rougirait,
Et qu'elle aurait longtemps, pour la cacher au monde,
    Dans un caveau mise au secret.

Pauvre ange, elle chantait, votre note criarde:
    «Que rien ici-bas n'est certain,
Et que toujours, avec quelque soin qu'il se farde,
    Se trahit l'égoïsme humain;

Que c'est un dur métier que d'être belle femme,
    Et que c'est le travail banal
De la danseuse folle et froide qui se pâme
    Dans un sourire machinal;

Que bâtir sur les cœurs est une chose sotte;
    Que tout craque, amour et beauté,
Jusqu'à ce que l'Oubli les jette dans sa hotte
    Pour les rendre à l'Eternité!»

....

From you, who are bright and joyous as a fanfare in the glittering morning, one plaintive note, one bizarre note that escaped, tottering

Like a child, a sickly, horrible, dark, unclean little girl, the shame of her family, who, to keep her from the eyes of the world, had long hidden her in some cellar.

Poor baby, she was singing, that harsh note of yours, and saying, 'That nothing here below is certain, and that always, however carefully it paints its face, human selfishness shows through;

'That it's a hard job being a beautiful woman; it's the repetitive work of the crazy, cold dancer swooning with her mechanical smile;

'That to build on hearts is a piece of folly, that everything breaks, love and beauty, until Forgetfulness gathers them up in his basket to take them back to Eternity.'

J'ai souvent évoqué cette lune enchantée,
        Ce silence et cette langueur,
Et cette confidence horrible chuchotée
        Au confessionnal du cœur.

32 (XLVI) L'Aube Spirituelle

Quand chez les débauchés l'aube blanche et vermeille
Entre en société de l'Idéal rongeur,
Par l'opération d'un mystère vengeur
Dans la brute assoupie un ange se réveille.

Des Cieux Spirituels l'inaccessible azur,
Pour l'homme terrassé que rêve encore et souffre,
S'ouvre et s'enfonce avec l'attirance du gouffre.
Ainsi, chère Déesse, Etre lucide et pur,

Sur les débris fumeux des stupides orgies
Ton souvenir plus clair, plus rose, plus charmant,
A mes yeux agrandis voltige incessamment.

....

I have often recalled that enchanted moon, that silence and that languor, and that horrible secret whispered in the confessional of the heart.

Spiritual Dawn

When to the lodgings of debauchees the pink and white dawn comes, accompanied by the gnawing Ideal, a vengeful mystery begins to operate: in the torpid brute an angel awakes.

Spiritual Skies in their inaccessible azure open to the earthbound man who still dreams and suffers, and recede before him with the magnetic pull of the abyss. So, dear Goddess, pure and lucid being,

On the smoking debris of crass orgies, the memory of you, brighter, rosier, more enchanting, hovers incessantly before my dilated eyes.

Le soleil a noirci la flamme des bougies;
Ainsi, toujours vainqueur, ton fantôme est pareil,
Ame resplendissante, à l'immortel soleil!

33 (XLVII) Harmonie du Soir

Voici venir les temps où vibrant sur sa tige
Chaque fleur s'évapore ainsi qu'un encensoir;
Les sons et les parfums tournent dans l'air du soir;
Valse mélancolique et langoureux vertige!

Chaque fleur s'évapore ainsi qu'un encensoir;
Le violon frémit comme un cœur qu'on afflige;
Valse mélancolique et langoureux vertige!
Le ciel est triste et beau comme un grand reposoir.

Le violon frémit comme un cœur qu'on afflige,
Un cœur tendre, qui hait le néant vaste et noir!
Le ciel est triste et beau comme un grand reposoir;
Le soleil s'est noyé dans son sang qui se fige.

....

The sun has darkened the flames of the candles; thus, ever victorious, your
phantom resembles, o resplendent soul, the immortal sun.

Evening Harmony

Now the times are coming when, vibrating on its stem, each flower rises in
vapour like an incense-burner; sounds and scents circle in the evening air,
melancholy waltz and languorous vertigo!

Each flower rises in vapour like an incense burner; the violin trembles like
a wounded heart; melancholy waltz and languorous vertigo! The sky is sad
and beautiful like a great altar of repose:

The violin trembles like a wounded heart, a tender heart which hates the
vast, black nothingness! The sky is sad and beautiful like a great altar of
repose; the sun has drowned in his curdling blood.

Un cœur tendre, qui hait le néant vaste et noir,
Du passé lumineux recueille tout vestige!
Le soleil s'est noyé dans son sang qui se fige . . .
Ton souvenir en moi luit comme un ostensoir!

34 (XLVIII) Le Flacon

Il est de forts parfums pour qui toute matière
Est poreuse. On dirait qu'ils pénètrent le verre.
En ouvrant un coffret venu de l'Orient
Dont la serrure grince et rechigne en criant,

Ou dans une maison déserte quelque armoire
Pleine de l'âcre odeur des temps, poudreuse et noire,
Parfois on trouve un vieux flacon qui se souvient,
D'où jaillit toute vive une âme qui revient.

....

A loving heart, which hates the vast, black nothingness, gathers up every
trace of the shining past! The sun has drowned in his curdling blood . . .
Your memory within me shines like a monstrance.

The Phial

In the presence of some strong perfumes all matter is porous. They seem to
penetrate even glass. On opening a casket brought from the Orient whose
lock creaks and protests loudly,
      Or, in a deserted house, some cupboard, full of the acrid smell of times
past, dusty and dark, sometimes we find an old scent bottle that remembers,
from which there springs, all alive, a returning soul.

Mille pensers dormaient, chrysalides funèbres,
Frémissant doucement dans les lourdes ténèbres,
Qui dégagent leur aile et prennent leur essor,
Teintés d'azur, glacés de rose, lamés d'or.

Voilà le souvenir enivrant qui voltige
Dans l'air troublé; les yeux se ferment; le Vertige
Saisit l'âme vaincue et la pousse à deux mains
Vers un gouffre obscurci de miasmes humains;

Il la terrasse au bord d'un gouffre séculaire,
Où, Lazare odorant déchirant son suaire,
Se meut dans son réveil le cadavre spectral
D'un vieil amour ranci, charmant et sépulcral.

Ainsi, quand je serai perdu dans la mémoire
Des hommes, dans le coin d'une sinistre armoire
Quand on m'aura jeté, vieux flacon désolé,
Décrépit, poudreux, sale, abject, visqueux, fêlé,

....

A thousand thoughts were sleeping, deathly chrysalids, trembling gently
in the heavy darkness, which now unfold their wings and take flight, tinged
with azure, glazed with pink, shot with gold.

Now here, in a rush, is memory, hovering in the uneasy air; eyes close;
dizziness seizes the vanquished soul and pushes her with both hands towards
a pit shrouded in human effluvia;

He throws her to the ground on the edge of a centuries-old pit in which,
like a stinking Lazarus bursting through his shroud, there moves, awakening,
the ghostly corpse of an old love, rancid, delightful and belonging to the
grave.

Even so, when I am lost in the memory of men, there in the corner of
some gloomy cupboard where I have been thrown, a sorry old phial,
decrepit, dusty, dirty, wretched, sticky, cracked,

Je serai ton cercueil, aimable pestilence!
Le témoin de ta force et de ta virulence,
Cher poison préparé par les anges! liqueur
Qui me ronge, ô la vie et la mort de mon cœur!

35 (XLIX) Le Poison

Le vin sait revêtir le plus sordide bouge
       D'un luxe miraculeux,
Et fait surgir plus d'un portique fabuleux
       Dans l'or de sa vapeur rouge,
Comme un soleil couchant dans un ciel nébuleux.

L'opium agrandit ce qui n'a pas de bornes,
       Allonge l'illimité,
Approfondit le temps, creuse la volupté,
       Et de plaisirs noirs et mornes
Remplit l'âme au-delà de sa capacité.

....

I shall be your coffin, beloved pestilence! the witness to your strength and to your virulence, dear poison mixed by the angels! liquor which is eating me away, o the life and the death of my heart!

Poison

Wine can clothe the most sordid den in miraculous luxury, and makes more than one fairy-tale portico rise up in the gold of its red vapours, like a setting sun in a misty sky.

    Opium enlarges that which is boundless, extends the unlimited, deepens time, digs further into pleasure, and fills the soul with black gloomy pleasures to its capacity and more.

Tout cela ne vaut pas le poison qui découle
    De tes yeux, de tes yeux verts,
Lacs où mon âme tremble et se voit à l'envers . . .
    Mes songes viennent en foule
Pour se désaltérer à ces gouffres amers.

Tout cela ne vaut pas le terrible prodige
    De ta salive qui mord,
Qui plonge dans l'oubli mon âme sans remords,
    Et, charriant le vertige,
La roule défaillante aux rives de la mort!

36 (LI) Le Chat

I

Dans ma cervelle se promène,
Ainsi qu'en son appartement,
Un beau chat, fort, doux et charmant.
Quand il miaule, on l'entend à peine,

....

All that is nothing compared to the poison which flows from your eyes,
from your green eyes, lakes where my soul trembles and sees itself upside
down . . . My dreams crowd to slake their thirst in those bitter gulfs.

All that is nothing, compared to the terrible prodigy of your biting saliva,
which plunges my soul into oblivion without remorse and, bearing vertigo
on its waves, casts it up fainting on the shores of death.

The Cat

I

In my brain there walks about, as if in his own rooms, a fine cat, strong,
gentle and delightful. When he miaows, you can hardly hear him,

Tant son timbre est tendre et discret;
Mais que sa voix s'apaise ou gronde,
Elle est toujours riche et profonde.
C'est là son charme et son secret.

Cette voix, qui perle et qui filtre
Dans mon fonds le plus ténébreux,
Me remplit comme un vers nombreux
Et me réjouit comme un philtre.

Elle endort les plus cruels maux
Et contient toutes les extases;
Pour dire les plus longues phrases,
Elle n'a pas besoin de mots.

Non, il n'est pas d'archet qui morde
Sur mon cœur, parfait instrument,
Et fasse plus royalement
Chanter sa plus vibrante corde,

Que ta voix, chat mystérieux,
Chat séraphique, chat étrange,
En qui tout est, comme en un ange,
Aussi subtil qu'harmonieux!

···

His tone is so tender and discreet; but whether his voice is peaceful or angry it is always rich and profound. That is his charm and his secret.

This voice, which seeps and trickles through my darkest depths, satisfies me like a rhythmical line of verse and fills me with joy like a philtre.

It dulls the cruellest pains and contains all ecstasies; to speak the longest sentences it does not need words.

No, there is no bow that can cut into my heart, that perfect instrument, and make its most resonant string sing more royally,

Than your voice, mysterious cat, seraphic cat, strange cat, in whom everything is, as in an angel, no less subtle than harmonious.

II

De sa fourrure blonde et brune
Sort un parfum si doux, qu'un soir
J'en fus embaumé, pour l'avoir
Caressée une fois, rien qu'une.

C'est l'esprit familier du lieu;
Il juge, il préside, il inspire
Toutes choses dans son empire;
Peut-être est-il fée, est-il dieu?

Quand mes yeux, vers ce chat que j'aime
Tirés comme par un aimant,
Se retournent docilement
Et que je regarde en moi-même,

Je vois avec étonnement
Le feu de ses prunelles pâles,
Clairs fanaux, vivantes opales,
Qui me contemplent fixement.

....

II

From his blond and brown fur comes a smell so sweet that one evening I
was all perfumed with it after having stroked him once, just once.

He is the familiar spirit of the place; he judges, he presides, he inspires
everything within his empire; perhaps he is a fairy, a god?

When my eyes, drawn as if by a magnet to this cat I love, turn again
docilely towards him, and when I look into myself,

I am astonished to see the fire of his pale eyes, bright beacons, living opals,
looking at me with a fixed gaze.

37 (LII) Le Beau Navire

Je veux te raconter, ô molle enchanteresse!
Les diverses beautés qui parent ta jeunesse;
      Je veux te peindre ta beauté,
Où l'enfance s'allie à la maturité.

Quand tu vas balayant l'air de ta jupe large,
Tu fais l'effet d'un beau vaisseau qui prend le large,
      Chargé de toile, et va roulant
Suivant un rythme doux, et paresseux, et lent.

Sur ton cou large et rond, sur tes épaules grasses,
Ta tête se pavane avec d'étranges grâces;
      D'un air placide et triomphant
Tu passes ton chemin, majestueuse enfant.

Je veux te raconter, ô molle enchanteresse!
Les diverses beautés qui parent ta jeunesse;
      Je veux te peindre ta béauté,
Où l'enfance s'allie à la maturité.

....

The Beautiful Ship

I want to tell you, o soft enchantress, of the varied beauties which adorn your young body; I wish to paint for you your beauty, where childhood joins with maturity.

When you go along, sweeping the air with your wide skirt, you have the look of a fine vessel putting out to sea, laden with sail, and rolling in a gentle rhythm, lazy and slow.

On your broad, round neck, on your plump shoulders, your head bears itself high, with strange, graceful airs; placid and triumphant, you go your way, majestic child.

I want . . .

Ta gorge que s'avance et qui pousse la moire,
Ta gorge triomphante est une belle armoire
      Dont les panneaux bombés et clairs
Comme les boucliers accrochent des éclairs;

Boucliers provocants, armés de pointes roses!
Armoire à doux secrets, pleine de bonnes choses,
      De vins, de parfums, de liqueurs
Qui feraient délirer les cerveaux et les cœurs!

Quand tu vas balayant l'air de ta jupe large,
Tu fais l'effet d'un beau vaisseau qui prend le large,
      Chargé de toile, et va roulant
Suivant un rythme doux, et paresseux, et lent.

Tes nobles jambes, sous les volants qu'elles chassent,
Tourmentent les désirs obscurs et les agacent,
      Comme deux sorcières qui font
Tourner un philtre noir dans un vase profond.

Tes bras, qui se joueraient des précoces hercules,
Sont des boas luisants les solides émules,
      Faits pour serrer obstinément,
Comme pour l'imprimer dans ton cœur, ton amant.

Your thrusting bosom, pushing at the silk, your triumphant bosom is a fine cupboard whose panels, convex and bright, are like shields catching shafts of light.

Provoking shields, armed with pink points! Cupboard with sweet secrets, full of good things, of wines, of perfumes, of cordials which would drive brains and hearts wild!

When you go along . . .

Your noble legs, under the flounces which they drive along, torment hidden desires and stir them up, like two witches turning a black philtre in a deep vessel.

Your arms, which would make short work of a precocious Hercules, are solid rivals to gleaming boa constrictors, made to squeeze your lover unyieldingly, as if to leave his impression on your heart.

Sur ton cou large et rond, sur tes épaules grasses,
Ta tête se pavane avec d'étranges grâces;
        D'un air placide et triomphant
Tu passes ton chemin, majestueuse enfant.

38 (LIII) L'Invitation au Voyage

      Mon enfant, ma sœur,
      Songe à la douceur
D'aller là-bas vivre ensemble!
      Aimer à loisir,
      Aimer et mourir
Au pays qui te ressemble!
      Les soleils mouillés
      De ces ciels brouillés
Pour mon esprit ont les charmes
      Si mystérieux
      De tes traîtres yeux,
Brillant à travers leurs larmes.

Là, tout n'est qu'ordre et beauté,
Luxe, calme et volupté.

....

On your broad, round neck . . .

The Invitation to the Voyage

Child, sister, think of the sweetness of going to that far country to live
together! To love at our leisure, to love and to die in the country which is
like you! The watery suns of those overcast skies have, for my spirit, the
same mysterious charm as your killing eyes, shining through their tears.
    There, there is nothing but order and beauty, luxury, calm and sensual
pleasure.

Des meubles luisants,
Polis par les ans,
Décoreraient notre chambre;
Les plus rares fleurs
Mêlant leurs odeurs
Aux vagues senteurs de l'ambre,
Les riches plafonds,
Les miroirs profonds,
La splendeur orientale,
Tout y parlerait
A l'âme en secret
Sa douce langue natale.

Là, tout n'est qu'ordre et beauté,
Luxe, calme et volupté.

Vois sur ces canaux
Dormir ces vaisseaux
Dont l'humeur est vagabonde; .
C'est pour assouvir
Ton moindre désir
Qu'ils viennent du bout du monde.

....

Shining furniture, polished by the years, would decorate our room; the
rarest flowers, mingling their scents with the vague perfume of ambergris;
the rich ceilings, the deep mirrors, the oriental splendour, everything would
speak to the soul in secret its sweet native tongue.

There . . .

See, on the canals, the vessels sleeping, their wandering humour stilled; it
is to satisfy your every desire that they have come from the ends of the
earth. The setting suns clothe the fields, the canals, the whole city, in
hyacinth and gold; the world is falling asleep in a warm light.

There . . .

– Les soleils couchants
Revêtent les champs,
Les canaux, la ville entière,
D'hyacinthe et d'or;
Le monde s'endort
Dans une chaude lumière.

Là, tout n'est qu'ordre et beauté,
Luxe, calme et volupté.

39 (LIV) L'Irréparable

Pouvons-nous étouffer le vieux, le long Remords,
        Qui vit, s'agite et se tortille,
Et se nourrit de nous comme le ver des morts,
        Comme du chêne la chenille?
Pouvons-nous étouffer l'implacable Remords?

Dans quel philtre, dans quel vin, dans quelle tisane,
        Noierons-nous ce vieil ennemi,
Destructeur et gourmand comme la courtisane,
        Patient comme la fourmi?
Dans quel philtre? – dans quel vin? – dans quelle tisane?

....

The Irreparable

Can we stifle that old, that long Remorse, who lives, moves, writhes and feeds on us as the worm on the dead? As the caterpillar on the oak tree? Can we stifle implacable Remorse?

In what philtre, in what wine, in what infusion shall we drown that old enemy, destructive and greedy as the courtesan, patient as the ant? In what philtre, in what wine, in what infusion?

Dis-le, belle sorcière, oh! dis, si tu le sais,
   A cet esprit comblé d'angoisse
Et pareil au mourant qu'écrasent les blessés,
   Que le sabot du cheval froisse,
Dis-le, belle sorcière, oh! dis, si tu le sais,

A cet agonisant que le loup déjà flaire
   Et que surveille le corbeau,
A ce soldat brisé! s'il faut qu'il désespère
   D'avoir sa croix et son tombeau;
Ce pauvre agonisant que déjà le loup flaire!

Peut-on illuminer un ciel bourbeux et noir?
   Peut-on déchirer des ténèbres
Plus denses que la poix, sans matin et sans soir,
   Sans astres, sans éclairs funèbres?
Peut-on illuminer un ciel bourbeux et noir?

L'Espérance qui brille aux carreaux de l'Auberge
   Est soufflée, est morte à jamais!
Sans lune et sans rayons, trouver où l'on héberge
   Les martyrs d'un chemin mauvais!
Le Diable a tout éteint aux carreaux de l'Auberge!

....

 Tell me, beautiful witch, speak, if you can, to this spirit overborne with anguish and like to the dying man being crushed by the wounded, bruised by the horse's hoof, tell him, beautiful witch, if you can,

 This dying man whom the wolf already scents, and over whom the crow keeps watch, this broken soldier! Say if he must despair of having his cross and his grave, poor dying wretch whom already the wolf scents!

 Can we light up a muddy, black sky? Can we tear through darkness thicker than pitch, without morning or evening, without stars, without funereal lightning? Can we light up a muddy, black sky?

 Hope which shines in the windows of the Inn has been blown out, is dead for ever! Without moon or rays, how to find a shelter for the martyrs of a wicked road? The Devil has doused all the lights in the windows of the Inn!

Adorable sorcière, aimes-tu les damnés?
        Dis, connais-tu l'irrémissible?
Connais-tu le Remords, aux traits empoisonnés,
        A qui notre cœur sert de cible?
Adorable sorcière, aimes-tu les damnés?

L'Irréparable ronge avec sa dent maudite
        Notre âme, piteux monument,
Et souvent il attaque, ainsi que le termite,
        Par la base le bâtiment.
L'Irréparable ronge avec sa dent maudite!

— J'ai vu parfois, au fond d'un théâtre banal
        Qu'enflammait l'orchestre sonore,
Une fée allumer dans un ciel infernal
        Une miraculeuse aurore;
J'ai vu parfois au fond d'un théâtre banal

Un être, qui n'était que lumière, or et gaze,
        Terrasser l'énorme Satan;
Mais mon cœur, que jamais ne visite l'extase,
        Est un théâtre où l'on attend
Toujours, toujours en vain, l'Etre aux ailes de gaze!

....

    Adorable witch, do you like damned people? Tell the truth, do you know the unforgivable sin? Do you know Remorse, with its poisoned arrows and our heart for its target? Adorable witch, do you like the damned?

    The Irreparable gnaws with its cursed tooth at our soul, that pitiful monument, and often, like the termite, it attacks the edifice from the base. The Irreparable gnaws with its cursed tooth!

    — I have sometimes seen, at the far end of a commonplace theatre, set on fire by the noise of the orchestra, a fairy light up a hellish sky with a miraculous dawn; I have sometimes seen, in a common theatre,

    A being made of nothing but light, gold and gauze strike down huge Satan; but my heart, which ecstasy never visits, is a theatre awaiting for ever, for ever and in vain, the Being with the gauzy wings.

40 (LVI) Chant d'Automne

I

Bientôt nous plongerons dans les froides ténèbres;
Adieu, vive clarté de nos étés trop courts!
J'entends déjà tomber avec des chocs funèbres
Le bois retentissant sur le pavé des cours.

Tout l'hiver va rentrer dans mon être: colère,
Haine, frissons, horreur, labeur dur et forcé,
Et, comme le soleil dans son enfer polaire,
Mon cœur ne sera plus qu'un bloc rouge et glacé.

J'écoute en frémissant chaque bûche qui tombe;
L'échafaud qu'on bâtit n'a pas d'écho plus sourd.
Mon esprit est pareil à la tour qui succombe
Sous les coups du bélier infatigable et lourd.

....

Autumn Song

I

Soon we shall be plunging into cold darkness; goodbye, living brightness of
our too-short summers! I already hear the deadly, echoing thud of logs
falling on the paving-stones of courtyards.

All winter will come back into my being: anger, hatred, shudders, horror,
hard, forced labour, and, like the sun in its polar hell, my heart will be no
more than a red, icy block.

I listen, trembling, to the fall of each log; the building of a scaffold does
not have a more hollow echo. My spirit is like the tower, giving way under
the blows of the battering-ram, tireless and heavy.

Il me semble, bercé par ce choc monotone,
Qu'on cloue en grande hâte un cercueil quelque part.
Pour qui? – C'était hier l'été; voici l'automne!
Ce bruit mystérieux sonne comme un départ.

II

J'aime de vos longs yeux la lumière verdâtre,
Douce beauté, mais tout aujourd'hui m'est amer,
Et rien, ni votre amour, ni le boudoir, ni l'âtre,
Ne me vaut le soleil rayonnant sur la mer.

Et pourtant aimez-moi, tendre cœur! soyez mère,
Même pour un ingrat, même pour un méchant;
Amante ou sœur, soyez la douceur éphémère
D'un glorieux automne ou d'un soleil couchant.

Courte tâche! La tombe attend; elle est avide!
Ah! laissez-moi, mon front posé sur vos genoux,
Goûter, en regrettant l'été blanc et torride,
De l'arrière-saison le rayon jaune et doux!

....

It seems to me, lulled by this monotonous pounding, that someone somewhere is hastily nailing down a coffin. For whom? Yesterday it was summer; now here is autumn! The mysterious sound seems to announce a departure.

II

I love your long eyes with their greenish light, gentle beauty, but everything is bitter to me today, and nothing, neither your love, nor the boudoir, nor the hearth can replace for me the light of the sun on the sea.

But still love me, tender heart! Be a mother even to an ungrateful child, even to someone wicked; mistress or sister, be the ephemeral sweetness of a glorious autumn or of a setting sun.

A short-lived task! The tomb awaits; it is greedy! Ah, let me lie with my head on your knees and taste, as I regret the passing of white, torrid summer, the yellow, soft light of the turn of the year.

41 (LVII) A une Madone

EX-VOTO DANS LE GOÛT ESPAGNOL

Je veux bâtir pour toi, Madone, ma maîtresse,
Un autel souterrain au fond de ma détresse,
Et creuser dans le coin le plus noir de mon cœur,
Loin du désir mondain et du regard moqueur,
Une niche, d'azur et d'or tout émaillée,
Où tu te dresseras, Statue émerveillée.
Avec mes Vers polis, treillis d'un pur métal
Savamment constellé de rimes de cristal,
Je ferai pour ta tête une énorme Couronne;
Et dans ma Jalousie, ô mortelle Madone,
Je saurai te tailler un Manteau, de façon
Barbare, roide et lourd, et doublé de soupçon,
Qui, comme une guérite, enfermera tes charmes;
Non de Perles brodé, mais de toutes mes Larmes!

....

To a Madonna
EX-VOTO IN THE SPANISH TASTE

I mean to build for you, Lady, my mistress, an underground altar in the
depths of my anguish, and to hollow out, in the blackest corner of my heart,
far from worldly desires and mocking eyes, a niche all enamelled in azure
and gold, where you will stand, a wonder-struck Statue. Of my polished
Verses, cunningly bestarred with crystal rhymes, I shall make for your head
an enormous Crown; and from my jealousy, o mortal Madonna, I shall
know how to cut for you a Cloak of barbarous fashion, stiff and heavy and
lined with suspicion, which will enclose your charms like a sentry-box; it
will be embroidered, not with Pearls but with all my Tears. Your Robe will

Ta Robe, ce sera mon Désir, frémissant,
Onduleux, mon Désir qui monte et qui descend,
Aux pointes se balance, aux vallons se repose,
Et revêt d'un baiser tout ton corps blanc et rose.
Je te ferai de mon Respect de beaux Souliers
De satin, par tes pieds divins humiliés,
Qui, les emprisonnant dans une molle étreinte,
Comme un moule fidèle en garderont l'empreinte.
Si je ne puis, malgré tout mon art diligent,
Pour Marchepied tailler une Lune d'argent,
Je mettrai le Serpent qui me mord les entrailles
Sous tes talons, afin que tu foules et railles,
Reine victorieuse et féconde en rachats,
Ce monstre tout gonflé de haine et de crachats.
Tu verras mes Pensers, rangés comme les Cierges
Devant l'autel fleuri de la Reine des Vierges,
Etoilant de reflets le plafond peint en bleu,
Te regarder toujours avec des yeux de feu;
Et comme tout en moi te chérit et t'admire,
Tout se fera Benjoin, Encens, Oliban, Myrrhe,
Et sans cesse vers toi, sommet blanc et neigeux,
En Vapeurs montera mon Esprit orageux.

....

be my Desire, trembling, undulating, my Desire which rises and falls,
perching on the peaks, resting in the valleys and clothing all your white and
pink body in a kiss. I will make for you from my Respect two fine Shoes of
satin, humbled beneath your divine feet and trapping them in a gentle grip,
keeping the shape of them like a faithful mould. If I cannot, despite all my
diligent art, cut out a silver Moon as your footstool, I shall put under your
heels the Serpent that bites my entrails so that you trample and mock him, o
victorious Queen, endless source of atonement, mock that monster all puffed
up with hatred and spittle. You will see my Thoughts, lined up like candles
before the flower-decked altar of the Queen of Virgins, starring the blue
ceiling with reflections and always watching you with eyes of fire; and as
everything in me cherishes and worships you, everything will become
Benzoin, Incense and Myrrh, and unceasingly towards you, as if to a white,
snowy summit, my stormy Spirit will rise in vapours.

Enfin, pour compléter ton rôle de Marie,
Et pour mêler l'amour avec la barbarie,
Volupté noire! des sept Péchés capitaux,
Bourreau plein de remords, je ferai sept Couteaux
Bien affilés, et, comme un jongleur insensible,
Prenant le plus profond de ton amour pour cible,
Je les planterai tous dans ton Cœur pantelant,
Dans ton Cœur sanglotant, dans ton Cœur ruisselant!

42 (LVIII) Chanson d'Après-Midi

Quoique tes sourcils méchants
Te donnent un air étrange
Qui n'est pas celui d'un ange,
Sorcière aux yeux alléchants,

Je t'adore, ô ma frivole,
Ma terrible passion!
Avec la dévotion
Du prêtre pour son idole.

....

Finally, to complete your role as Mary, and to mingle love with barbarity, black delight! from the seven deadly Sins, I shall, an executioner filled with remorse, make seven well-honed Knives, and like an unheeding juggler, taking the deepest springs of your love as my target, I shall plant every one of them in your panting Heart, in your sobbing Heart, in your streaming Heart!

Afternoon Song

Although your wicked eyebrows give you a strange look which is not that of an angel, witch with the alluring eyes,

I adore you, o my frivolous, my terrifying passion, with the devotion of a priest for his idol.

Le désert et la forêt
Embaument tes tresses rudes,
Ta tête a les attitudes
De l'énigme et du secret.

Sur ta chair le parfum rôde
Comme autour d'un encensoir;
Tu charmes comme le soir,
Nymphe ténébreuse et chaude.

Ah! les philtres les plus forts
Ne valent pas ta paresse,
Et tu connais la caresse
Qui fait revivre les morts!

Tes hanches sont amoureuses
De ton dos et de tes seins,
Et tu ravis les coussins
Par tes poses langoureuses.

Quelquefois, pour apaiser
Ta rage mystérieuse,
Tu prodigues, sérieuse,
La morsure et le baiser;

....

The desert and the forest lend their scents to your rough tresses, your head has the angles of enigma and secret.

About your flesh perfume hovers as if around a censer; you cast a spell like evening, hot and shadowy nymph.

Ah, the strongest philtres cannot equal your lazy charm, and you know the caress that brings the dead back to life.

Your hips are in love with your back and your breasts, and you excite the cushions with your languorous poses.

Sometimes, to calm your mysterious fury, you cover me, with a serious look, in bites and kisses;

Tu me déchires, ma brune,
Avec un rire moqueur,
Et puis tu mets sur mon cœur
Ton œil doux comme la lune.

Sous tes souliers de satin,
Sous tes charmants pieds de soie,
Moi, je mets ma grande joie,
Mon génie et mon destin,

Mon âme par toi guérie,
Par toi, lumière et couleur!
Explosion de chaleur
Dans ma noire Sibérie!

43 (LXII) Mœsta et Errabunda

Dis-moi, ton cœur parfois s'envole-t-il, Agathe,
Loin du noir océan de l'immonde cité,
Vers un autre océan où la splendeur éclate,
Bleu, clair, profond, ainsi que la virginité?
Dis-moi, ton cœur parfois s'envole-t-il, Agathe?

....

You tear me apart, dark beauty, with a mocking laugh, and then you lay upon my heart your look, gentle as the moon.

Under your satin shoes, under your charming silken feet, I place my greatest joy, my genius and my destiny,

My soul cured by you, by you, light and colour! Explosion of heat in my black Siberia!

Moesta et Errabunda

Tell me, does your heart ever fly away, Agatha, far from the black ocean of the filthy city, towards another ocean where light explodes, blue, bright, deep as virginity? Tell me, does your heart sometimes fly away, Agatha?

La mer, la vaste mer, console nos labeurs!
Quel démon a doté la mer, rauque chanteuse
Qu'accompagne l'immense orgue des vents grondeurs,
De cette fonction sublime de berceuse?
La mer, la vaste mer, console nos labeurs!

Emporte-moi, wagon! enlève-moi, frégate!
Loin! loin! ici la boue est faite de nos pleurs!
— Est-il vrai que parfois le triste cœur d'Agathe
Dise: Loin des remords, des crimes, des douleurs,
Emporte-moi, wagon, enlève-moi, frégate?

Comme vous êtes loin, paradis parfumé,
Où sous clair azur tout n'est qu'amour et joie,
Où tout ce que l'on aime est digne d'être aimé,
Où dans la volupté pure le cœur se noie!
Comme vous êtes loin, paradis parfumé!

Mais le vert paradis des amours enfantines,
Les courses, les chansons, les baisers, les bouquets,
Les violons vibrant derrière les collines,
Avec les brocs de vin, le soir, dans les bosquets,
— Mais le vert paradis des amours enfantines,

....

The sea, the vast sea consoles our labours! What demon has endowed the sea, hoarse singer accompanied by the immense organ of the growling winds, with that sublime function of cradling us? The sea, the vast sea consoles our labours!

Take me away, wagon! carry me off, frigate! Far, far away! Here the mud is made of our tears! Is it true that sometimes Agatha's sad heart says, 'Take me away, wagon! carry me off, frigate!'?

How far away you are, perfumed paradise, where under a clear blue sky there is nothing but love and joy, where everything one loves is worthy of being loved, where pure pleasure floods the heart? How far away you are, perfumed paradise!

But the green paradise of childish loves, the songs, the kisses, the posies of flowers, the violins throbbing behind the hills with the jugs of wine, at evening, in the glades — But the green paradise of childish loves,

L'innocent paradis, plein de plaisirs furtifs,
Est-il déjà plus loin que l'Inde et que la Chine?
Peut-on le rappeler avec des cris plaintifs,
Et l'animer encor d'une voix argentine,
L'innocent paradis plein de plaisirs furtifs?

44 (LXVI) Les Chats

Les amoureux fervents et les savants austères
Aiment également, dans leur mûre saison,
Les chats puissants et doux, orgueil de le maison,
Qui comme eux sont frileux et comme eux sédentaires.

Amis de la science et de la volupté,
Ils cherchent le silence et l'horreur des ténèbres;
L'Erèbe les eût pris pour ses coursiers funèbres,
S'ils pouvaient au servage incliner leur fierté.

....

That innocent paradise, full of furtive pleasures, is it already further away than India and than China? Can we call it back with plaintive cries and bring it alive once more with a silvery voice, that innocent paradise full of furtive pleasures?

Cats

Fervent lovers and austere scholars both, in their riper years, love cats, those powerful, soft creatures, the pride of the house, who like them hate the cold and like them are sedentary.

Friends to knowledge and to pleasure, they seek the silence and shivers of darkness; Erebus would have taken them for its messengers of death if they could bend their pride to servitude.

Ils prennent en songeant les nobles attitudes
Des grands sphinx allongés au fond des solitudes,
Qui semblent s'endormir dans un rêve sans fin;

Leurs reins féconds sont pleins d'étincelles magiques,
Et des parcelles d'or, ainsi qu'un sable fin,
Etoilent vaguement leurs prunelles mystiques.

45 (LXXV) Spleen

Pluviôse, irrité contre la ville entière,
De son urne à grands flots verse un froid ténébreux
Aux pâles habitants du voisin cimetière
Et la mortalité sur les faubourgs brumeux.

Mon chat sur le carreau cherchant une litière
Agite sans repos son corps maigre et galeux;
L'âme d'un vieux poète erre dans la gouttière
Avec la triste voix d'un fantôme frileux.

....

They assume in sleep the noble attitudes of the great sphinxes, stretched out in the furthest places of solitude, who seem to be falling asleep in an endless dream;

Their fertile loins are full of magic sparks, and flecks of gold, like a fine sand, sparkle like vague stars in their mystic pupils.

Spleen

Pluviôse, angry with the whole city, is pouring down from his urn a great flood of chilly darkness upon the pale inhabitants of the nearby cemetery, and raised death rates upon the foggy inner suburbs.

My cat, seeking a sleeping place on the bare floor, restlessly shifts his thin, mangy body; the soul of an old poet is wandering in the roof gutters with the sad voice of a shivering ghost.

Le bourdon se lamente, et la bûche enfumée
Accompagne en fausset la pendule enrhumée,
Cependant qu'en un jeu plein de sales parfums,

Héritage fatal d'une vieille hydropique,
Le beau valet de cœur et la dame de pique
Causent sinistrement de leurs amours défunts.

46 (LXXVI) Spleen

J'ai plus de souvenirs que si j'avais mille ans.

Un gros meuble à tiroirs encombré de bilans,
De vers, de billets doux, de procès, de romances,
Avec de lourds cheveux roulés dans des quittances,
Cache moins de secrets que mon triste cerveau.
C'est une pyramide, un immense caveau,
Qui contient plus de morts que la fosse commune.
— Je suis un cimetière abhorré de la lune,

....

The great bell complains, and the smoking log sings a falsetto accompaniment to the wheezy clock, while in a pack of cards full of dirty smells,

Sinister legacy of a dropsical old woman, the handsome knave of hearts and the queen of clubs talk ominously of their dead loves.

Spleen

I have more memories than if I were a thousand years old.

A big piece of furniture, a chest of drawers cluttered with balance sheets, with verses, love-letters, lawsuits, ballads, with heavy locks of hair rolled up in receipted bills, hides fewer secrets than my wretched brain. It is a pyramid, an enormous burial vault that holds more dead than the paupers' field. I am a graveyard shunned by the moon, where, like fits of remorse,

Où comme des remords se traînent de longs vers
Qui s'acharnent toujours sur mes morts les plus chers.
Je suis un vieux boudoir plein de roses fanées,
Où gît tout un fouillis de modes surannées,
Où les pastels plaintifs et les pâles Boucher,
Seuls, respirent l'odeur d'un flacon débouché.

Rien n'égale en longueur les boiteuses journées,
Quand sous les lourds flocons des neigeuses années
L'ennui, fruit de la morne incuriosité,
Prend les proportions de l'immortalité.
– Désormais tu n'es plus, ô matière vivante!
Qu'un granit entouré d'une vague épouvante,
Assoupi dans le fond d'un Sahara brumeux;
Un vieux sphinx ignoré du monde insoucieux,
Oublié sur la carte, et dont l'humeur farouche
Ne chante qu'aux rayons du soleil qui se couche.

....

long worms slither and always choose to feed on my dearest dead. I am an
old boudoir full of withered roses, where lie disorderly heaps of out-of-date
fashions, where the plaintive pastels and faded Bouchers alone breathe in the
odour of an unstoppered scent bottle.

Nothing equals the length of the limping days, when, under the heavy
flakes of the snowy years, tedium, born of dull incuriosity, takes on the
proportions of immortality. Now you are no longer, o living matter,
anything but a block of granite surrounded by a formless fear, lying torpid
in the furthest reaches of a misty Sahara; an old sphinx unregarded by the
careless world, forgotten on the map, and whose unsociable whim it is to
sing only to the rays of the setting sun.

47 (LXXVII) Spleen

Je suis comme le roi d'un pays pluvieux,
Riche, mais impuissant, jeune et pourtant très vieux,
Qui, de ses précepteurs méprisant les courbettes,
S'ennuie avec ses chiens comme avec d'autres bêtes.
Rien ne peut l'égayer, ni gibier, ni faucon,
Ni son peuple mourant en face du balcon.
Du bouffon favori la grotesque ballade
Ne distrait plus le front de ce cruel malade;
Son lit fleurdelisé se transforme en tombeau,
Et les dames d'atour, pour qui tout prince est beau,
Ne savent plus trouver d'impudique toilette
Pour tirer un souris de ce jeune squelette.
. Le savant qui lui fait de l'or n'a jamais pu
De son être extirper l'élément corrompu,

....

Spleen

I am like the king of a rainy country, rich but powerless, young and yet
very old, who, despising the bowing and scraping of his tutors, bores
himself in the company of his dogs, as of other creatures. Nothing can cheer
him, neither game nor falcon, nor his people dying within view of his
balcony. The favourite buffoon with his grotesque ballad can no longer
lighten the brow of the cruel invalid; his fleur-de-lis-draped bed is turning
into a tomb, and the ladies-in-waiting, for whom any prince is handsome,
can no longer think of any shameless costume to draw a smile from the
young skeleton. The learned man who makes gold for him has never
managed to extirpate the corrupt element from his being, and even in those

Et dans ces bains de sang qui des Romains nous viennent,
Et dont sur leurs vieux jours les puissants se souviennent,
Il n'a su réchauffer ce cadavre hébété
Où coule au lieu de sang l'eau verte du Léthé.

48 (LXXVIII) Spleen

Quand le ciel bas et lourd pèse comme un couvercle
Sur l'esprit gémissant en proie aux longs ennuis,
Et que de l'horizon embrassant tout le cercle
Il nous verse un jour noir plus triste que les nuits;

Quand la terre est changée en un cachot humide,
Où l'Espérance, comme une chauve-souris,
S'en va battant les murs de son aile timide
Et se cognant la tête à des plafonds pourris;

....

baths of blood which come down to us from the Romans, and which, in their old age, the powerful begin to remember, he has not been able to warm up that unfeeling corpse in which, instead of blood, runs the green water of Lethe.

Spleen

When the low, heavy sky weighs like a lid on the spirit as it groans in the grip of long tedium, and when, filling the whole circle of the horizon, it pours out upon us a black daylight more gloomy than nights;

When the earth is changed to a damp dungeon where Hope, like a bat, flies about beating its timid wings against the walls and bumping its head on rotten ceilings;

Quand la pluie étalant ses immenses traînées
D'une vaste prison imite les barreaux,
Et qu'un peuple muet d'infâmes araignées
Vient tendre ses filets au fond de nos cerveaux,

Des cloches tout à coup sautent avec furie
Et lancent vers le ciel un affreux hurlement,
Ainsi que des esprits errants et sans patrie
Qui se mettent à geindre opiniâtrement.

— Et de longs corbillards, sans tambours ni musique,
Défilent lentement dans mon âme; l'Espoir,
Vaincu, pleure, et l'Angoisse atroce, despotique,
Sur mon crâne incliné plante son drapeau noir.

....

When the rain, dragging out its immense, oblique lines, mimics the bars
of a vast prison, and a silent tribe of filthy spiders comes to spin its webs in
the depths of our brains;

Bells suddenly leap furiously to life and set up a ghastly howling to
heaven, like wandering, homeless spirits beginning to moan unstoppably.

— And long funeral processions, without drums or music, file past slowly
in my soul; Hope, defeated, weeps, and cruel, despotic anguish plants its
black flag in my bowed skull.

49 (LXXXI) Alchimie de la Douleur

L'un t'éclaire avec son ardeur,
L'autre en toi met son deuil, Nature!
Ce qui dit à l'un: Sépulture!
Dit à l'autre: Vie et splendeur!

Hermès inconnu qui m'assistes
Et qui toujours m'intimidas,
Tu me rends l'égal de Midas,
Le plus triste des alchimistes;

Par toi je change l'or en fer
Et le paradis en enfer;
Dans le suaire des nuages

Je découvre un cadavre cher,
Et sur les célestes rivages
Je bâtis de grands sarcophages.

....

Alchemy of Sorrow

One man lights you up with his ardour, the other puts all his mourning into
you, o Nature! What says to the one, 'Burial', says to the other, 'Life and
splendour!'

Unknown Hermes who helps me and who has always intimidated me,
you make me the equal of Midas, saddest of all alchemists;

With your help I turn gold into iron and heaven into hell; in the shroud
of the clouds

I discover a beloved corpse, and on the heavenly shores I build great
sarcophagi.

50 (LXXXII) Horreur Sympathique

De ce ciel bizarre et livide,
Tourmenté comme ton destin,
Quels pensers dans ton âme vide
Descendent? réponds, libertin.

– Insatiablement avide
De l'obscur et de l'incertain,
Je ne geindrai pas comme Ovide
Chassé du paradis latin.

Cieux déchirés comme des grèves,
En vous se mire mon orgueil;
Vos vastes nuages en deuil

Sont les corbillards de mes rêves,
Et vos lueurs sont le reflet
De l'Enfer où mon cœur se plaît.

....

Sympathetic Horror

From that bizarre, livid sky, tormented like your destiny, what thoughts
descend into your empty soul? Answer, unbeliever.

Insatiably drawn to the obscure and uncertain, I shall not moan like Ovid,
expelled from the Latin paradise.

Skies torn like seashores, in you my pride contemplates itself; your vast,
mourning-black clouds

Are the hearses of my dreams, and your shafts of light are the reflections
of Hell, where my heart is at home.

51 (LXXXIII) L'Héautontimorouménos

A J.G.F.

Je te frapperai sans colère
Et sans haine, comme un boucher,
Comme Moïse le rocher!
Et je ferai de ta paupière,

Pour abreuver mon Sahara,
Jaillir les eaux de la souffrance.
Mon désir gonflé d'espérance
Sur tes pleurs salés nagera

Comme un vaisseau qui prend le large,
Et dans mon cœur qu'ils soûleront
Tes chers sanglots retentiront
Comme un tambour qui bat la charge!

Ne suis-je pas un faux accord
Dans la divine symphonie,
Grâce à la vorace Ironie
Qui me secoue et qui me mord?

....

The Heautontimoroumenos

I will strike you without anger and without hatred, like a butcher, like Moses striking the rock! And from your eyelids,

To slake my Sahara, I will make spring the waters of suffering. My desire, swelled with hope, will swim on your salt tears

Like a ship putting out to sea, and in my heart, which will be drunk with them, your dear sobs will resound like a drum beating the charge!

Am I not a discord in the divine symphony, because of the voracious Irony that shakes me and gnaws me?

Elle est dans ma voix, la criarde!
C'est tout mon sang, ce poison noir!
Je suis le sinistre miroir
Où la mégère se regarde.

Je suis la plaie et le couteau!
Je suis le soufflet et la joue!
Je suis les membres et la roue,
Et la victime et le bourreau!

Je suis de mon cœur le vampire,
– Un de ces grands abandonnés
Au rire éternel condamnés,
Et qui ne peuvent plus sourire!

52 (LXXXIV) L'Irrémédiable

I

Une Idée, une Forme, un Etre
Parti de l'azur et tombé
Dans un Styx bourbeux et plombé
Où nul œil du Ciel ne pénètre;

....

She is there in my voice, the shrill creature! It is all of my blood, that black poison. I am the ill-omened mirror where the shrew watches herself.

I am the wound and the knife! I am the blow and the cheek! I am the limbs and the wheel, and the victim and the torturer!

I am the vampire of my own heart – one of those great outcasts condemned to eternal laughter and who can no longer smile.

The Irremediable

I

An Idea, a Form, a Being, come from on high and fallen into a muddy, leaden Styx where no eye of Heaven can penetrate;

Un Ange, imprudent voyageur
Qu'a tenté l'amour du difforme,
Au fond d'un cauchemar énorme
Se débattant comme un nageur,

Et luttant, angoisses funèbres!
Contre un gigantesque remous
Qui va chantant comme les fous
Et pirouettant dans les ténèbres;

Un malheureux ensorcelé
Dans ses tâtonnements futiles,
Pour fuir d'un lieu plein de reptiles,
Cherchant la lumière et la clé;

Un damné descendant sans lampe,
Au bord d'un gouffre dont l'odeur
Trahit l'humide profondeur,
D'éternels escaliers sans rampe,

Où veillent des monstres visqueux
Dont les larges yeux de phosphore
Font une nuit plus noire encore
Et ne rendent visibles qu'eux;

....

An Angel, unwary traveller tempted by the love of the misshapen, caught
in a huge nightmare and struggling like a swimmer,
   And fighting, deadly anguish, against a gigantic eddy that goes by singing
as madmen do and pirouetting in the darkness;
   An unfortunate, bewitched, groping futilely, trying to escape from a place
full of reptiles, looking for the light and the key;
   A damned man without a lamp, on the edge of a pit whose smell betrays
its damp depth, going down endless stairs without a rail,
   Where slimy monsters are watching, whose wide, phosphorescent eyes
make the night even darker and allow only themselves to be seen;

Un navire pris dans le pôle,
Comme en un piège de cristal,
Cherchant par quel détroit fatal
Il est tombé dans cette geôle;

– Emblèmes nets, tableau parfait
D'une fortune irrémédiable,
Qui donne à penser que le Diable
Fait toujours bien tout ce qu'il fait!

II

Tête-à-tête sombre et limpide
Qu'un cœur devenu son miroir!
Puits de Vérité, clair et noir,
Où tremble une étoile livide,

Un phare ironique, infernal,
Flambeau des grâces sataniques,
Soulagement et gloire uniques,
– La conscience dans le Mal!

....

A ship caught in the pole, as in a crystal trap, trying to guess by what fatal channel it strayed into this gaol;
– Clear emblems, perfect image of an irremediable fate, which leads one to think that the Devil does well whatever he does.

II

Dark, limpid tête-à-tête of a heart become its own mirror. Well of Truth, clear and black, where one livid star trembles,
One ironic, hellish beacon, torch of Satan's graces, the only comfort and the only glory: consciousness in Evil.

TABLEAUX PARISIENS

(Parisian Pictures)

53 (LXXXIX) Le Cygne

A Victor Hugo

I

Andromaque, je pense à vous! Ce petit fleuve,
Pauvre et triste miroir où jadis resplendit
L'immense majesté de vos douleurs de veuve,
Ce Simoïs menteur qui par vos pleurs grandit,

A fécondé soudain ma mémoire fertile,
Comme je traversais le nouveau Carrousel.
Le vieux Paris n'est plus (la forme d'une ville
Change plus vite, hélas! que le cœur d'un mortel);

....

The Swan

I

Andromache, I am thinking of you! That little river, poor, sad mirror in
which there once shone forth the immense majesty of your widow's sorrow,
that false Simois that swelled with your tears,

Suddenly flooded over my fertile memory, as I was crossing the new
Carrousel! The old Paris is no more; the shape of a city changes faster, alas,
than a human heart;

Je ne vois qu'en esprit tout ce camp de baraques,
Ces tas de chapiteaux ébauchés et de fûts,
Les herbes, les gros blocs verdis par l'eau des flaques,
Et, brillant aux carreaux, le bric-à-brac confus.

Là s'étalait jadis une ménagerie;
Là je vis, un matin, à l'heure où sous les cieux
Froids et clairs le Travail s'éveille, où la voirie
Pousse un sombre ouragan dans l'air silencieux,

Un cygne qui s'était évadé de sa cage,
Et, de ses pieds palmés frottant le pavé sec,
Sur le sol raboteux traînait son blanc plumage.
Près d'un ruisseau sans eau la bête ouvrant le bec

Baignait nerveusement ses ailes dans la poudre,
Et disait, le cœur plein de son beau lac natal:
«Eau, quand donc pleuvras-tu? quand tonneras-tu, foudre?»
Je vois ce malheureux, mythe étrange et fatal,

....

I see only in the mind's eye that camp of shacks, those piles of roughed-out capitals and sections of columns, the weeds, the great blocks turning green in the water of the puddles, and, reflected in the windows, the nameless jumble.

That was the site of a menagerie; there I saw, one morning, at the hour when under the cold, clear sky work is stirring, when the dustcarts send up a dark hurricane into the silent air,

A swan that had escaped from its cage, and, rubbing its webbed feet on the dry pavement, was dragging its white plumage on the rough ground. Near a dry gutter the creature, opening its beak,

Was nervously bathing its wings in the dust, and saying, its heart full of its beautiful native lake, 'Water, when will you rain down? When will you thunder, o lightning?' I see the poor wretch, strange and ineluctable myth,

Vers le ciel quelquefois, comme l'homme d'Ovide,
Vers le ciel ironique et cruellement bleu,
Sur son cou convulsif tendant sa tête avide,
Comme s'il adressait des reproches à Dieu!

II

Paris change! mais rien dans ma mélancolie
N'a bougé! palais neufs, échafaudages, blocs,
Vieux faubourgs, tout pour moi devient allégorie,
Et mes chers souvenirs sont plus lourds que des rocs.

Aussi devant ce Louvre une image m'opprime:
Je pense à mon grand cygne, avec ses gestes fous,
Comme les exilés, ridicule et sublime,
Et rongé d'un désir sans trêve! et puis à vous,

Andromaque, des bras d'un grand époux tombée,
Vil bétail, sous la main du superbe Pyrrhus,
Auprès d'un tombeau vide en extase courbée;
Veuve d'Hector, hélas! et femme d'Hélénus!

....

Sometimes reach towards the sky, like Ovid's man, towards the ironic, cruelly blue sky, stretching its greedy head on its convulsive neck, as if it were reproaching God.

II

Paris changes! But nothing in my melancholy has moved! New palaces, scaffolding, blocks, old, settled districts, everything for me becomes an allegory, and my dear memories are heavier than boulders.

So in front of this same Louvre an image oppresses me: I think of my great swan, with his mad gestures, like an exile, ridiculous and sublime, and consumed by an unrelenting desire, and then of you,

Andromache, fallen from the arms of a mighty spouse, now wretched cattle under the hand of proud Pyrrhus, bowed in a trance next to an empty tomb, widow of Hector, alas, and wife to Helenus.

Je pense à la négresse, amaigrie et phtisique,
Piétinant dans la boue, et cherchant, l'œil hagard,
Les cocotiers absents de la superbe Afrique
Derrière la muraille immense du brouillard;

A quiconque a perdu ce qui ne se retrouve
Jamais, jamais! à ceux qui s'abreuvent de pleurs
Et tettent la Douleur comme une bonne louve!
Aux maigres orphelins séchant comme des fleurs!

Ainsi dans la forêt où mon esprit s'exile
Un vieux Souvenir sonne à plein souffle du cor!
Je pense aux matelots oubliés dans une île,
Aux captifs, aux vaincus! . . . à bien d'autres encor!

....

I think of the negress, wasted and consumptive, trampling in the mud and
looking with wild eyes for the missing coconut palms of proud Africa
behind the immense wall of the fog;

Of whoever has lost what can never be found again, never! Of those
whose drink is tears, who suck at sorrow like a kindly she-wolf! Of thin
orphans withering like flowers!

And in the forest where my spirit wanders and is lost, an old Memory
sounds its horn at full blast. I think of sailors, forgotten on some island, of
captives, of the defeated . . . of many others yet.

54 (XC) Les Sept Vieillards

A Victor Hugo

Fourmillante cité, cité pleine de rêves,
Où le spectre en plein jour raccroche le passant!
Les mystères partout coulent comme des sèves
Dans les canaux étroits du colosse puissant.

Un matin, cependant que dans la triste rue
Les maisons, dont la brume allongeait la hauteur,
Simulaient les deux quais d'une rivière accrue,
Et que, décor semblable à l'âme de l'acteur,

Un brouillard sale et jaune inondait tout l'espace,
Je suivais, roidissant mes nerfs comme un héros
Et discutant avec mon âme déjà lasse,
Le faubourg secoué par les lourds tombereaux.

....

The Seven Old Men

Swarming city, city full of dreams, where ghosts in broad daylight catch the walker's sleeve. Mysteries everywhere run like sap through the narrow channels of the powerful colossus.

One morning, while in the dull street the houses, their height accentuated by the mist, seemed like the two banks of a river in spate, and, scenery well suited to the soul of the actor,

A dirty yellow fog flooded all around, I was following, stiffening my sinews like a hero and arguing with my already weary soul, the path of the heavy tumbrils as they shook the old district.

Tout à coup, un vieillard dont les guenilles jaunes
Imitaient la couleur de ce ciel pluvieux,
Et dont l'aspect aurait fait pleuvoir les aumônes,
Sans la méchanceté qui luisait dans ses yeux,

M'apparut. On eût dit sa prunelle trempée
Dans le fiel; son regard aiguisait les frimas,
Et sa barbe à longs poils, roide comme une épée,
Se projetait, pareille à celle de Judas.

Il n'était pas voûté, mais cassé, son échine
Faisant avec sa jambe un parfait angle droit,
Si bien que son bâton, parachevant sa mine,
Lui donnait la tournure et le pas maladroit

D'un quadrupède infirme ou d'un juif à trois pattes.
Dans la neige et la boue il allait s'empêtrant,
Comme s'il écrasait des morts sous ses savates,
Hostile à l'univers plutôt qu'indifférent.

....

Suddenly, an old man whose yellow rags matched the colour of the rainy
sky, and whose appearance would have made alms rain upon him, were it
not for the malevolence that gleamed in his eyes,

Appeared to me. You would have thought his pupils had been dipped in
gall; his look sharpened the frost; and his beard with its long hairs, stiff as a
sword, stuck out like Judas's.

He was not just stooped, but bent double, his spine making a perfect right
angle with his legs, so that his stick, completing his appearance, gave him
the shape and the clumsy gait

Of an injured quadruped or a three-legged Jew. On he came, his feet
sticking in the snow and mud, as if he were crushing dead men under his old
shoes, hostile to the universe rather than indifferent.

Son pareil le suivait: barbe, œil, dos, bâton, loques,
Nul trait ne distinguait, du même enfer venu,
Ce jumeau centenaire, et ces spectres baroques
Marchaient du même pas vers un but inconnu.

A quel complot infâme étais-je donc en butte,
Ou quel méchant hasard ainsi m'humiliait?
Car je comptai sept fois, de minute en minute,
Ce sinistre vieillard qui se multipliait!

Que celui-là qui rit de mon inquiétude,
Et qui n'est pas saisi d'un frisson fraternel,
Songe bien que malgré tant de décrépitude
Ces sept monstres hideux avaient l'air éternel!

Aurais-je, sans mourir, contemplé le huitième,
Sosie inexorable, ironique et fatal,
Dégoûtant Phénix, fils et père de lui-même?
– Mais je tournai le dos au cortège infernal.

....

Another like him was following him: beard, eye, back, stick, rags,
nothing distinguished his centenarian twin, come from the same hell, and
these outlandish ghosts were walking at the same pace towards an unknown
goal.

Of what vile plot was I the victim, or what wicked chance was humiliating
me in this way? For I counted seven times, from minute to minute, that
sinister old man who was replicating himself!

Let anyone who laughs at my anxiety, and who is not seized by a
sympathetic shudder, reflect that in spite of their extreme decrepitude, those
seven hideous monsters had a look of eternity about them!

Would I have been able to see, and live, the eighth inexorable double,
ironic and inescapable, disgusting Phoenix, son and father to himself? – But
I turned my back on the hellish procession.

Exaspéré comme un ivrogne qui voit double,
Je rentrai, je fermai ma porte, épouvanté,
Malade et morfondu, l'esprit fiévreux et trouble,
Blessé par le mystère et par l'absurdité!

Vainement ma raison voulait prendre la barre;
La tempête en jouant déroutait ses efforts,
Et mon âme dansait, dansait vieille gabarre
Sans mâts, sur une mer monstrueuse et sans bords!

55 (XCI) Les Petites Vieilles

A Victor Hugo

I

Dans les plis sinueux des vieilles capitales,
Où tout, même l'horreur, tourne aux enchantements,
Je guette, obéissant à mes humeurs fatales,
Des êtres singuliers, décrépits et charmants.

....

Infuriated, like a drunkard seeing double, I went home and closed my
door, terrified, ill and chilled to the bone, my spirit feverish and troubled,
wounded by mystery and absurdity.

In vain my reason tried to take the helm, the tempest played with it and
foiled all its efforts, and my soul tossed, tossed, an old, dismasted lighter, on
a monstrous, shoreless sea!

Little Old Ladies

I

In the sinuous folds of old capital cities, where everything, even horror, turns
to magic, I am constantly on the watch, driven by my ineluctable whims,
for certain singular beings, decrepit and delightful.

Ces monstres disloqués furent jadis des femmes,
Eponine ou Laïs! Monstres brisés, bossus
Ou tordus, aimons-les! ce sont encor des âmes.
Sous des jupons troués et sous de froids tissus

Ils rampent, flagellés par les bises iniques,
Frémissant au fracas roulant des omnibus,
Et serrant sur leur flanc, ainsi que des reliques,
Un petit sac brodé de fleurs ou de rébus;

Ils trottent, tout pareils à des marionnettes;
Se traînent, comme font les animaux blessés,
Ou dansent, sans vouloir danser, pauvres sonnettes
Où se pend un Démon sans pitié! Tout cassés

Qu'ils sont, ils ont des yeux perçants comme une vrille,
Luisants comme ces trous où l'eau dort dans la nuit;
Ils ont les yeux divins de la petite fille
Qui s'étonne et qui rit à tout ce qui reluit.

....

These disjointed monsters were once women, Eponina or Lais! Monsters though they be, broken, hunchbacked or twisted, let us love them! They are still souls. Under holed petticoats and under cold, thin stuffs

They crawl, whipped by the cruel winds, trembling at the loud rumble of the omnibuses, and clutching to their sides, like relics, a little purse embroidered with flowers or ciphers;

They trot along, just like marionettes; drag themselves like wounded animals, or dance without wanting to dance, poor bells on whose rope a pitiless demon hangs! All broken

As they are, they have eyes as sharp as gimlets, shining like those holes where water sleeps at night; they have the godlike eyes of the baby girl, surprised and laughing at anything that glitters.

– Avez-vous observé que maints cercueils de vieilles
Sont presque aussi petits que celui d'un enfant?
La Mort savante met dans ces bières pareilles
Un symbole d'un goût bizarre et captivant,

Et lorsque j'entrevois un fantôme débile
Traversant de Paris le fourmillant tableau,
Il me semble toujours que cet être fragile
S'en va tout doucement vers un nouveau berceau;

A moins que, méditant sur la géométrie,
Je ne cherche, à l'aspect de ces membres discords,
Combien de fois il faut que l'ouvrier varie
La forme de la boîte où l'on met tous ces corps.

– Ces yeux sont des puits faits d'un million de larmes,
Des creusets qu'un métal refroidi pailleta . . .
Ces yeux mystérieux ont d'invincibles charmes
Pour celui que l'austère Infortune allaita!

....

– Have you ever noticed that many old women's coffins are almost as small as a child's? Death in its wisdom makes of these similar biers a symbol in bizarre and captivating taste.

And when I see a frail ghost crossing Paris's swarming scene, I always think that the fragile being is going away quietly towards a new cradle;

Unless, my mind turning towards geometry, I ponder instead, looking at these ill-assorted limbs, how many times the workman must have to vary the shape of the box where all these bodies are put. –

Those eyes are wells made of a million tears, crucibles where metal now cold once sparkled . . . Those mysterious eyes have an irresistible charm for one whom stern Misfortune suckled!

II

De Frascati défunt Vestale enamourée;
Prêtresse de Thalie, hélas! dont le souffleur
Enterré sait le nom; célèbre evaporée
Que Tivoli jadis ombragea dans sa fleur,

Toutes m'enivrent; mais parmi ces êtres frêles
Il en est qui, faisant de la douleur un miel,
Ont dit au Dévouement qui leur prêtait ses ailes:
Hippogriffe puissant, mène-moi jusqu'au ciel!

L'une, par sa patrie au malheur exercée,
L'autre, que son époux surchargea de douleurs,
L'autre, par son enfant Madone transpercée,
Toutes auraient pu faire un fleuve avec leurs pleurs!

III

Ah! que j'en ai suivi de ces petites vieilles!
Une, entre autres, à l'heure. où le soleil tombant
Ensanglante le ciel de blessures vermeilles,
Pensive, s'asseyait à l'écart sur un banc,

....

II

The Vestal in love with long-dead Frascatis; the priestess of Thalia, whose
name the prompter, now buried, knows; the fashionable feather-brain
whom Tivoli's shades knew in her springtime;

They all intoxicate me; but among these frail beings there are some who,
turning sorrow into honey, said to the Self-sacrifice that lent them its wings,
'Mighty Hippogriff, carry me to heaven!'

One, trained by her country in suffering, another, whom her husband
overloaded with sorrows, another, a Madonna pierced through by her child,
all of them could have made a river with their tears!

III

I have followed so many of those little old ladies! One, among others, at the
time when the setting sun makes the sky bloody with rosy wounds, would
pensively sit apart on the edge of the crowd, on a bench,

Pour entendre un de ces concerts, riches de cuivre,
Dont les soldats parfois inondent nos jardins,
Et qui, dans ces soirs d'or où l'on se sent revivre,
Versent quelque héroïsme au cœur des citadins.

Celle-là, droite encor, fière et sentant la règle,
Humait avidement ce chant vif et guerrier;
Son œil parfois s'ouvrait comme l'œil d'un vieil aigle;
Son front de marbre avait l'air fait pour le laurier!

IV

Telles vous cheminez, stoïques et sans plaintes,
A travers le chaos des vivantes cités,
Mères au cœur saignant, courtisanes ou saintes,
Dont autrefois les noms par tous étaient cités.

Vous qui fûtes la grâce ou qui fûtes la gloire,
Nul ne vous reconnaît! un ivrogne incivil
Vous insulte en passant d'un amour dérisoire;
Sur vos talons gambade un enfant lâche et vil.

....

To hear one of those concerts, rich in brass, with which the soldiers sometimes flood our parks, and which, in those golden evenings when one feels oneself come back to life, instil some heroism into the hearts of city-dwellers.

The old lady, still upright and conscious of proper bearing, was eagerly sniffing up that lively, warlike melody. Her eye sometimes opened like the eye of an old eagle; her marble brow seemed made for a laurel wreath!

IV

So you make your way, stoical and without complaint, through the chaos of living cities, mothers with bleeding hearts, courtesans or saints, whose names once were known to all.

You who were grace and you who were glory, no one recognizes you! A rude drunkard insults you as you pass with a jeering offer of love; at your heels prances a cowardly, cruel child.

Honteuses d'exister, ombres ratatinées,
Peureuses, le dos bas, vous côtoyez les murs;
Et nul ne vous salue, étranges destinées!
Débris d'humanité pour l'éternité mûrs!

Mais moi, moi qui de loin tendrement vous surveille,
L'œil inquiet, fixé sur vos pas incertains,
Tout comme si j'étais votre père, ô merveille!
Je goûte à votre insu des plaisirs clandestins:

Je vois s'épanouir vos passions novices;
Sombres ou lumineux, je vis vos jours perdus;
Mon cœur multiplié jouit de tous vos vices!
Mon âme resplendit de toutes vos vertus!

Ruines! ma famille! ô cerveaux congénères!
Je vous fais chaque soir un solennel adieu!
Où serez-vous demain, Eves octogénaires,
Sur qui pèse la griffe effroyable de Dieu?

....

Ashamed to exist, shrivelled shadows, frightened, your backs bent, you keep to the wall; and no one greets you, strange destinies! Ruins of humanity, ripe for the next world!

But I, I who watch you tenderly from a distance, keeping a worried eye on your uncertain steps, as if I were your father, how astonishing! I enjoy secret pleasures without your knowledge.

I see your earliest passions unfold; I live your lost days, dark or filled with light; my heart, taking on multiple identities, enjoys all your vices! My soul shines forth with all your virtues!

Ruins! my family! o fellow brains! I say a solemn adieu to you every evening! Where will you be tomorrow, octogenarian Eves, over whom hangs the terrible claw of God?

56 (XCIV) Le Squelette Laboureur

I

Dans les planches d'anatomie
Qui traînent sur ces quais poudreux
Où maint livre cadavéreux
Dort comme une antique momie,

Dessins auxquels la gravité
Et le savoir d'un vieil artiste,
Bien que le sujet en soit triste,
Ont communiqué la Beauté,

On voit, ce qui rend plus complètes
Ces mystérieuses horreurs,
Bêchant comme des laboureurs,
Des Ecorchés et des Squelettes.

....

The Digging Skeleton

I

In the anatomical plates that lie around on those dusty embankments where
the corpse of many a book sleeps like an ancient mummy,

Drawings which the seriousness and the knowledge of an old artist,
despite their sad subjects, have endowed with beauty,

We see, making these mysterious horrors even more complete, flayed
figures and skeletons digging like farm workers.

II

De ce terrain que vous fouillez,
Manants résignés et funèbres,
De tout l'effort de vos vertèbres,
Ou de vos muscles dépouillés,

Dites, quelle moisson étrange,
Forçats arrachés au charnier,
Tirez-vous, et de quel fermier
Avez-vous à remplir la grange?

Voulez-vous (d'un destin trop dur
Epouvantable et clair emblème!)
Montrer que dans la fosse même
Le sommeil promis n'est pas sûr;

Qu'envers nous le Néant est traître;
Que tout, même la Mort, nous ment,
Et que sempiternellement,
Hélas! il nous faudra peut-être

Dans quelque pays inconnu
Ecorcher la terre revêche
Et pousser une lourde bêche
Sous notre pied sanglant et nu?

....

II

From this earth that you are digging so thoroughly, resigned villeins of death, with all the effort of your vertebrae or your exposed sinews;

Say, what strange harvest, work-gang pressed from the charnel-house, do you gather, and what farmer is expecting you to fill his barn?

Are you trying to show (clear and dreadful emblem of a too-cruel fate!) that even in the grave the promised sleep is not certain;

That the Void betrays us; that everything, even Death, lies to us, and that for all eternity, alas! we shall perhaps,

In some unknown country, be obliged to flay the stubborn earth, and to push a heavy spade under our naked, bleeding foot?

57 (xcv) Le Crépuscule du Soir

Voici le soir charmant, ami du criminel;
Il vient comme un complice, à pas de loup; le ciel
Se ferme lentement comme une grande alcôve,
Et l'homme impatient se change en bête fauve.
O soir, aimable soir, désiré par celui
Dont les bras, sans mentir, peuvent dire: Aujourd'hui
Nous avons travaillé! – C'est le soir qui soulage
Les esprits que dévore une douleur sauvage,
Le savant obstiné dont le front s'alourdit,
Et l'ouvrier courbé qui regagne son lit.
Cependant des démons malsains dans l'atmosphère
S'éveillent lourdement, comme des gens d'affaire,
Et cognent en volant les volets et l'auvent.
A travers les lueurs que tourmente le vent
La Prostitution s'allume dans les rues;
Comme une fourmilière elle ouvre ses issues;
Partout elle se fraye un occulte chemin,
Ainsi que l'ennemi qui tente un coup de main;

....

Evening Twilight

Here is charming evening, the criminal's friend; he comes like an accomplice,
loping stealthily; the sky closes slowly like a great alcove, and impatient man
turns into a wild beast. O evening, sweet evening, longed for by him whose
arms can truthfully say: Today, we worked. Evening alone comforts spirits
devoured by a savage grief; the persistent scholar whose head droops
towards his page, and the workman, his back bent, heading towards his bed.
Meanwhile unhealthy demons in the atmosphere are sluggishly awakening,
like people with business to do, and, in their flight, are bumping into
shutters and porches. Amid the gleams that flicker in the wind Prostitution
is lighting up in the streets; like an anthill it is opening up its byways;
everywhere the whore is making her secret way, like an enemy preparing a
sudden attack; she moves in the bowels of the city of mud like a worm

Elle remue au sein de la cité de fange
Comme un ver qui dérobe à l'Homme ce qu'il mange.
On entend çà et là les cuisines siffler,
Les théâtres glapir, les orchestres ronfler;
Les tables d'hôte, dont le jeu fait les délices,
S'emplissent de catins et d'escrocs, leurs complices,
Et les voleurs, qui n'ont ni trêve ni merci,
Vont bientôt commencer leur travail, eux aussi,
Et forcer doucement les portes et les caisses
Pour vivre quelques jours et vêtir leurs maîtresses.

Recueille-toi, mon âme, en ce grave moment,
Et ferme ton oreille à ce rugissement.
C'est l'heure où les douleurs des malades s'aigrissent!
La sombre Nuit les prend à la gorge; ils finissent
Leur destinée et vont vers le gouffre commun;
L'hôpital se remplit de leurs soupirs. – Plus d'un
Ne viendra plus chercher la soupe parfumée,
Au coin du feu, le soir, auprès d'une âme aimée.

Encore la plupart n'ont-ils jamais connu
La douceur du foyer et n'ont jamais vécu!

....

stealing from Man what he eats. Here and there one can hear kitchens
seething, theatres yelping, orchestras rumbling; restaurants where gambling
is the main attraction are filling up with tarts and card-sharps, their accom-
plices, and the thieves, who know neither rest or mercy, will soon begin
their work too, and gently force doors and safes to live for a few days and
clothe their mistresses.

Reflect a while, my soul, at this grave moment, and stop your ears to all
this roaring. It is the hour when the pains of the sick grow sharper! Dark
Night catches them by the throat; they finish their destiny and go towards
the common gulf; the hospital fills with their sighs. More than one will
never return to claim his fragrant soup, in the evening, by the fireside, next
to a beloved soul.

And what is more, most of them have never known the comfort of a
home and have never lived!

58 (XCIX)

Je n'ai pas oublié, voisine de la ville,
Notre blanche maison, petite mais tranquille;
Sa Pomone de plâtre et sa vieille Vénus
Dans un bosquet chétif cachant leurs membres nus,
Et le soleil, le soir, ruisselant et superbe,
Qui, derrière la vitre où se brisait sa gerbe,
Semblait, grand œil ouvert dans le ciel curieux,
Contempler nos dîners longs et silencieux,
Répandant largement ses beaux reflets de cierge
Sur la nappe frugale et les rideaux de serge.

59 (C)

La servante au grand cœur dont vous étiez jalouse,
Et qui dort son sommeil sous une humble pelouse,
Nous devrions pourtant lui porter quelques fleurs.
Les morts, les pauvres morts, ont de grandes douleurs,

....

58

I have not forgotten it: near to the city, our white house, small but peaceful;
its plaster Pomona and its elderly Venus hiding their naked limbs in a
stunted copse, and the sun in the evening, splendidly streaming, there,
behind the window which broke its light into rays, and seeming like a great
eye open in the curious sky, looking down on our long silent dinners, and
spreading the largesse of its beautiful light, like that of altar candles, on the
frugal tablecloth and the serge curtains.

59

The great-hearted servant you were so jealous of, who is sleeping her sleep
out now under a humble patch of grass, we really should take her some

Et quand Octobre souffle, émondeur des vieux arbres,
Sont vent mélancolique à l'entour de leurs marbres,
Certe, ils doivent trouver les vivants bien ingrats,
A dormir, comme ils font, chaudement dans leurs draps,
Tandis que, dévorés de noires songeries,
Sans compagnon de lit, sans bonnes causeries,
Vieux squelettes gelés travaillés par le ver,
Ils sentent s'égoutter les neiges de l'hiver
Et le siècle couler, sans qu'amis ni famille
Remplacent les lambeaux qui pendent à leur grille.

Lorsque la bûche siffle et chante, si le soir,
Calme, dans le fauteuil je la voyais s'asseoir,
Si, par une nuit bleue et froide de décembre,
Je la trouvais tapie en un coin de ma chambre,
Grave, et venant du fond de son lit éternel
Couver l'enfant grandi de son œil maternel,
Que pourrais-je répondre à cette âme pieuse,
Voyant tomber des pleurs de sa paupière creuse?

---

flowers. The dead, the poor dead suffer terribly, and when October, pruner of old trees, blows his melancholy gusts round their marble monuments, they must surely find the living very ungrateful, to sleep, as they do, warmly between their sheets, while, eaten up with black dreams, with no bed-mates, no cosy chats, old frozen skeletons fretted by the worm, they feel the snows of winter drip away and time seep past, while no friends or family come to replace the scraps that hang from their plot railings.

When the log whistles and sings, if one evening, calm, I were to see her sit down in the armchair; if, one cold, blue December night I were to find her crouching in a corner of my room, solemn and come from the depths of her eternal bed to keep a mother's eye on the grown child; what could I say to that faithful soul, seeing tears fall from her hollow eyelids?

60 (CII) Rêve Parisien

A Constantin Guys

I

De ce terrible paysage,
Tel que jamais mortel n'en vit,
Ce matin encore l'image,
Vague et lointaine, me ravit.

Le sommeil est plein de miracles!
Par un caprice singulier,
J'avais banni de ces spectacles
Le végétal irrégulier,

Et, peintre fier de mon génie,
Je savourais dans mon tableau
L'enivrante monotonie
Du métal, du marbre et de l'eau.

....

Paris Dream

I

Of that terrible landscape, such as eye of man never saw, even the image, vague and distant this morning, is enough to ravish me.

Sleep is full of miracles! By a singular whim, I had banished from those scenes everything vegetable and irregular,

And, a painter proud of my genius, savoured in my picture the intoxicating monotony of metal, marble and water.

Babel d'escaliers et d'arcades,
C'était un palais infini,
Plein de bassins et de cascades
Tombant dans l'or mat ou bruni;

Et des cataractes pesantes,
Comme des rideaux de cristal,
Se suspendaient, éblouissantes,
A des murailles de métal.

Non d'arbres, mais de colonnades
Les étangs dormants s'entouraient,
Où de gigantesques naïades,
Comme des femmes, se miraient.

Des nappes d'eau s'épanchaient, bleues,
Entre des quais roses et verts,
Pendant des millions de lieues,
Vers les confins de l'univers;

C'étaient des pierres inouïes
Et des flots magiques; c'étaient
D'immenses glaces éblouies
Par tout ce qu'elles reflétaient!

....

A Babel of stairways and arcades, it was a palace of infinite size, full of
basins and waterfalls tumbling into matt or burnished gold;

And heavy cataracts, like crystal curtains, hung, dazzling bright, from
metal walls.

No trees, but colonnades surrounded the sleeping ponds, where gigantic
naiads, like women, gazed at their reflections.

Surfaces of water stretched away, blue, between pink and green quays, for
millions of miles, to the ends of the universe;

There were unheard-of stones and magic waves; there were enormous
mirrors, dazzled by what they reflected.

Insouciants et taciturnes,
Des Ganges, dans le firmament,
Versaient le trésor de leurs urnes
Dans des gouffres de diamant.

Architecte de mes féeries,
Je faisais, à ma volonté,
Sous un tunnel de pierreries
Passer un océan dompté;

Et tout, même la couleur noire,
Semblait fourbi, clair, irisé;
Le liquide enchâssait sa gloire
Dans le rayon cristallisé.

Nul astre d'ailleurs, nuls vestiges
De soleil, même au bas du ciel,
Pour illuminer ces prodiges,
Qui brillaient d'un feu personnel!

Et sur ces mouvantes merveilles
Planait (terrible nouveauté!
Tout pour l'œil, rien pour les oreilles!)
Un silence d'éternité.

....

Heedless and unspeaking, new Ganges, in the firmament, poured the
treasures of their urns into diamond gulfs.

The architect of my own magic scenery, I mastered an ocean and made it
flow, at my will, through a tunnel cut in jewels.

And everything, even the colour black, seemed burnished, bright, irides-
cent; the glory of liquid was contained within a setting of crystallized light.

No stars by the way, no sign of a sun, even low in the sky, to light up
these wonders, which shone with their own fires!

And over these ever-moving marvels there hung (terrifying novelty!
everything for the eye, nothing for the ears!) an eternal silence.

II

En rouvrant mes yeux pleins de flamme
J'ai vu l'horreur de mon taudis,
Et senti, rentrant dans mon âme,
La pointe des soucis maudits;

La pendule aux accents funèbres
Sonnait brutalement midi,
Et le ciel versait des ténèbres
Sur le triste monde engourdi.

61 (CIII) Le Crépuscule du Matin

La diane chantait dans les cours des casernes,
Et le vent du matin soufflait sur les lanternes.

C'était l'heure où l'essaim des rêves malfaisants
Tord sur leurs oreillers les bruns adolescents;
Où, comme un œil sanglant qui palpite et qui bouge,
La lampe sur le jour fait une tache rouge;

....

II

As I opened my eyes full of flame, I saw the horror of the slum where I live, and felt, entering my soul once more, the iron of my cursed cares;
    The clock with its deathly voice was brutally striking midday, and the sky was pouring down darkness on the sad, sluggish world.

Morning Twilight

Reveille was sounding in the barrack squares, and the morning wind was blowing on the lanterns.

    It was the hour when the swarm of malicious dreams makes brown boys twist and turn on their pillows; when, like a bloody eye throbbing and shifting, the lamp makes a red blur on the daylight; when the soul, beneath

Où l'âme, sous le poids du corps revêche et lourd,
Imite les combats de la lampe et du jour.
Comme un visage en pleurs que les brises essuient,
L'air est plein du frisson des choses qu's'enfuient,
Et l'homme est las d'écrire et la femme d'aimer.

Les maisons çà et là commençaient à fumer.
Les femmes de plaisir, la paupière livide,
Bouche ouverte, dormaient de leur sommeil stupide;
Les pauvresses, traînant leurs seins maigres et froids,
Soufflaient sur leurs tisons et soufflaient sur leurs doigts.
C'était l'heure où parmi le froid et la lésine
S'aggravent les douleurs des femmes en gésine;
Comme un sanglot coupé par un sang écumeux
Le chant du coq au loin déchirait l'air brumeux;
Une mer de brouillards baignait les édifices,
Et les agonisants dans le fond des hospices
Poussaient leur dernier râle en hoquets inégaux.
Les débauchés rentraient, brisés par leurs travaux.

---

the weight of the reluctant, heavy body, imitates the struggling between the lamp and the daylight. Like a weeping face, dried by the breezes, the air is full of the shiver of fleeing things, and man is tired of writing and woman of loving.

The houses here and there were beginning to smoke. Women of pleasure, their eyelids bruised, their mouths open, were sleeping their stupid sleep; female paupers, dragging their thin, cold breasts, were blowing on their embers and blowing on their fingers. It was the hour when, amid cold and miserliness, the pains of women in childbed grow worse; like a sob cut off by foaming blood, the cry of the cock in the distance tore the misty air; a sea of fog washed against the buildings; and the dying in the depths of the poorhouses were giving their death-rattle in irregular gulps. The debauchees were heading home, broken by their labours.

L'aurore grelottante en robe rose et verte
S'avançait lentement sur la Seine déserte,
Et le sombre Paris, en se frottant les yeux,
Empoignait ses outils, vieillard laborieux.

....

Dawn, shivering in a pink and green dress, was advancing slowly over the deserted Seine, and sombre Paris, rubbing its eyes, was picking up its tools, a hard-working old man.

LE VIN

(*Wine*)

62 (CVI) Le Vin de l'Assassin

Ma femme est morte, je suis libre!
Je puis donc boire tout mon soûl.
Lorsque je rentrais sans un sou,
Ses cris me déchiraient la fibre.

Autant qu'un roi je suis heureux;
L'air est pur, le ciel admirable . . .
Nous avions un été semblable
Lorsque j'en devins amoureux!

L'horrible soif qui me déchire
Aurait besoin pour s'assouvir
D'autant de vin qu'en peut tenir
Son tombeau; – ce n'est pas peu dire:

....

The Murderer's Wine

My wife's dead, I am free! Now I can drink as much as I want. When I used to come home broke, her yelling tore my nerves to pieces.

I'm as happy as a king; the air is clear, the sky is wonderful . . . We had a summer like this the year I fell in love with her.

The horrible thirst that's tearing me apart would need, in order to satisfy it, all the wine that her grave would hold – and that's saying something:

Je l'ai jetée au fond d'un puits,
Et j'ai même poussé sur elle
Tous les pavés de la margelle.
– Je l'oublierai si je le puis!

Au nom des serments de tendresse,
Dont rien ne peut nous délier,
Et pour nous réconcilier
Comme au beau temps de notre ivresse,

J'implorai d'elle un rendez-vous,
Le soir, sur une route obscure.
Elle y vint! – folle créature!
Nous sommes tous plus ou moins fous!

Elle était encore jolie,
Quoique bien fatiguée! et moi,
Je l'aimais trop! voilà pourquoi
Je lui dis: Sors de cette vie!

Nul ne peut me comprendre. Un seul
Parmi ces ivrognes stupides
Songea-t-il dans ses nuits morbides
A faire du vin un linceul?

....

I threw her down a well, and I even pushed over on to her all the coping-stones of the wall. I'll forget her now if I can.

In the name of all the vows of love we'd made that nothing could undo, and so as to get back together again like in the happy days when we were drunk with love,

I begged her to meet me one night, on a dark road. She came! She must have been mad, poor thing! Well, we're all more or less mad!

She was still pretty, though so tired-looking! and I loved her too much! That's why I said to her: 'Out of this life!'

No one can understand me. Did a single one among those stupid drunks ever dream, in the course of his sickly nights, of making wine into a shroud?

Cette crapule invulnérable
Comme les machines de fer
Jamais, ni l'été ni l'hiver,
N'a connu l'amour véritable,

Avec ses noirs enchantements,
Son cortège infernal d'alarmes,
Ses fioles de poison, ses larmes,
Ses bruits de chaîne et d'ossements!

— Me voilà libre et solitaire!
Je serai ce soir ivre mort;
Alors, sans peur et sans remords,
Je me coucherai sur la terre,

Et je dormirai comme un chien!
Le chariot aux lourdes roues
Chargé de pierres et de boues,
Le wagon enragé peut bien

Ecraser ma tête coupable
Ou me couper par le milieu,
Je m'en moque comme de Dieu,
Du Diable ou de la Sainte Table!

....

That bunch of scum, with no more feeling than iron machines, they've
never, winter or summer, known real love,
  With its black spells, its hellish train of sudden fears, its flasks of poison, its
tears, its dragging chains and rattling bones.
  So here I am, free and on my own! Tonight I'll be blind drunk; then,
without fear and without remorse, I'll lie down on the ground,
  And I'll sleep like a dog! The cart with its heavy wheels, laden with mud
and stones, the raging wagon can
  Crush my guilty head or cut me in two, I don't give a damn for them
any more than for God, the Devil or the Communion Table.

63 (CVIII) Le Vin des Amants

Aujourd'hui l'espace est splendide!
Sans mors, sans éperons, sans bride,
Partons à cheval sur le vin
Pour un ciel féerique et divin!

Comme deux anges que torture
Une implacable calenture,
Dans le bleu cristal du matin
Suivons le mirage lointain!

Mollement balancés sur l'aile
Du tourbillon intelligent,
Dans un délire parallèle,

Ma sœur, côte à côte nageant,
Nous fuirons sans repos ni trêves
Vers le paradis de mes rêves!

....

The Lover's Wine

Today space is magnificent! Without bit, without spurs, without bridle, let
us gallop away on the back of wine for a fairy-like, godlike sky!

Like two angels tortured by an implacable calenture, let us fly into the
blue crystal of morning in pursuit of the distant mirage!

Borne gently on the wing of the understanding whirlwind, in parallel
delirium,

O my sister, swimming side by side, we shall flee without rest or halt
towards the paradise of my dreams.

FLEURS DU MAL

(*Flowers of Evil*)

64 (CXI) Femmes Damnées

Comme un bétail pensif sur le sable couchées,
Elles tournent leurs yeux vers l'horizon des mers,
Et leurs pieds se cherchant et leurs mains rapprochées
Ont de douces langueurs et des frissons amers.

Les unes, cœurs épris des longues confidences,
Dans le fond des bosquets où jasent les ruisseaux,
Vont épelant l'amour des craintives enfances
Et creusent le bois vert des jeunes arbrisseaux;

D'autres, comme des sœurs, marchent lentes et graves
A travers les rochers pleins d'apparitions,
Où saint Antoine a vu surgir comme des laves
Les seins nus et pourprés de ses tentations;

....

Lost Women

Like pensive cattle lying on the sand, they turn their eyes towards the horizon of the seas, and their feet as they reach for each other and their joining hands feel sweet languors and bitter shiverings.

Some, hearts in love with long, confidential talks, walk in the depths of copses where streams babble, telling over the loves of apprehensive childhood, and cut into the green wood of young shrubs.

Others, like sisters, walk slowly and solemnly among rocks peopled with apparitions, where Saint Anthony saw rising up, like boiling lava, the naked, crimson-tinged breasts of his temptations.

Il en est, aux lueurs des résines croulantes,
Qui dans le creux muet des vieux antres païens
T'appellent au secours de leurs fièvres hurlantes,
O Bacchus, endormeur des remords anciens!

Et d'autres, dont la gorge aime les scapulaires,
Qui, recélant un fouet sous leurs longs vêtements,
Mêlent, dans le bois sombre et les nuits solitaires,
L'écume du plaisir aux larmes des tourments.

O vierges, ô démons, ô monstres, ô martyres,
De la réalité grands esprits contempteurs,
Chercheuses d'infini, dévotes et satyres,
Tantôt pleines de cris, tantôt pleines de pleurs,

Vous que dans votre enfer mon âme a poursuivies,
Pauvres sœurs, je vous aime autant que je vous plains,
Pour vos mornes douleurs, vos soifs inassouvies,
Et les urnes d'amour dont vos grands cœurs sont pleins!

....

There are some who, by the light of melting resin torches, in the silent hollows of old pagan caves, call on your help in their howling fevers, o Bacchus, duller of ancient remorse!

And others, whose bosoms love the scapular, who, hiding a whip under their long garments, mingle, in the dark wood and in solitary nights, the foam of pleasure with the tears of tortures.

O virgins, o devils, o monsters, o martyrs! Great souls contemptuous of reality, seekers of the infinite, saints and satyresses, now full of cries, now full of tears,

You whom my soul has pursued into your own hell, poor sisters, I love you as much as I pity you, for your bleak sufferings, your unquenched thirsts, and the springs of love with which your great hearts are full.

65 (CXII) Les Deux Bonnes Sœurs

La Débauche et la Mort sont deux aimables filles,
Prodigues de baisers et riches de santé,
Dont le flanc toujours vierge et drapé de guenilles
Sous l'éternel labeur n'a jamais enfanté.

Au poète sinistre, ennemi des familles,
Favori de l'enfer, courtisan mal renté,
Tombeaux et lupanars montrent sous leurs charmilles
Un lit que le remords n'a jamais fréquenté.

Et la bière et l'alcôve en blasphèmes fécondes
Nous offrent tour à tour, comme deux bonnes sœurs,
De terribles plaisirs et d'affreuses douceurs.

Quand veux-tu m'enterrer, Débauche aux bras immondes?
O Mort, quand viendras-tu, sa rivale en attraits,
Sur ses myrtes infects enter tes noirs cyprès?

....

The Two Good Sisters

Debauchery and Death are two good-hearted girls, free with their kisses and rich in good health, whose loins, ever virgin and draped in rags, though eternally ploughed, have never borne fruit.

To the sinister poet, enemy of families, favourite of hell, ill-provided courtier, tombs and brothels offer, under their arbours, a bed where remorse has never laid its head.

And the bier and the alcove abounding in blasphemies offer us in turn, like two kind sisters, terrible pleasures and hideous sweetnesses.

When will you bury me, o Debauchery of the unclean arms? O Death, her rival in attraction, when will you come and, upon her stinking myrtle, graft your black cypress boughs?

66 (CXIII) La Fontaine de Sang

Il me semble parfois que mon sang coule à flots,
Ainsi qu'une fontaine aux rythmiques sanglots.
Je l'entends bien qui coule avec un long murmure,
Mais je me tâte en vain pour trouver la blessure.

A travers la cité, comme dans un champ clos,
Il s'en va, transformant les pavés en îlots,
Désaltérant la soif de chaque créature,
Et partout colorant en rouge la nature.

J'ai demandé souvent à des vins captieux
D'endormir pour un jour la terreur qui me mine;
Le vin rend l'œil plus clair et l'oreille plus fine!

J'ai cherché dans l'amour un sommeil oublieux;
Mais l'amour n'est pour moi qu'un matelas d'aiguilles
Fait pour donner à boire à ces cruelles filles!

....

The Fountain of Blood

I sometimes feel that my blood is flowing in waves, like a fountain with its rhythmical sobs. I can hear it clearly, flowing with a long, murmuring sound, but I touch my body in vain to find the wound.

Through the city, as if in an enclosed arena, it goes, turning the paving-stones into islets, slaking the thirst of every creature and everywhere colouring nature red.

I have often asked heady wines to numb for a day the terror which eats away at me; wine makes the eye clearer and the ears sharper!

I have sought forgetful sleep in love; but love is nothing but a mattress of needles, made to give those cruel girls something to drink!

67 (CXVI) Un Voyage à Cythère

Mon cœur, comme un oiseau, voltigeait tout joyeux
Et planait librement à l'entour des cordages;
Le navire roulait sous un ciel sans nuages,
Comme un ange enivré d'un soleil radieux.

Quelle est cette île triste et noire? – C'est Cythère,
Nous dit-on, un pays fameux dans les chansons,
Eldorado banal de tous les vieux garçons.
Regardez, après tout, c'est une pauvre terre.

– Ile des doux secrets et des fêtes du cœur!
De l'antique Vénus le superbe fantôme
Au-dessus de tes mers plane comme un arôme,
Et charge les esprits d'amour et de langueur.

Belle île aux myrtes verts, pleine de fleurs écloses,
Vénérée à jamais par toute nation,
Où les soupirs des cœurs en adoration
Roulent comme l'encens sur un jardin de roses

....

A Voyage to Cythera

My heart, like a bird, was hovering joyously and circling freely around the rigging; the ship was rolling under a cloudless sky like an angel drunk on radiant sunlight.

What is that black, gloomy island? – It is Cythera, they said, a land famous in songs, the banal Eldorado of all old bachelors. Look: after all, it's not much of a place.

– Isle of sweet secrets and joys of the heart! The proud ghost of the Venus of antiquity floats like a perfume above your seas, filling minds with love and languor.

Fair isle of green myrtles, covered in full-blown flowers, ever venerated by all peoples, where the sighs of adoring hearts waft like incense over a rose garden,

Ou le roucoulement éternel d'un ramier!
– Cythère n'était plus qu'un terrain des plus maigres,
Un désert rocailleux troublé par des cris aigres.
J'entrevoyais pourtant un objet singulier!

Ce n'était pas un temple aux ombres bocagères,
Où la jeune prêtresse, amoureuse des fleurs,
Allait, le corps brûlé de secrètes chaleurs,
Entrebâillant sa robe aux brises passagères;

Mais voilà qu'en rasant la côte d'assez près
Pour troubler les oiseaux avec nos voiles blanches,
Nous vîmes que c'était un gibet à trois branches,
Du ciel se détachant en noir, comme un cyprès.

De féroces oiseaux perchés sur leur pâture
Détruisaient avec rage un pendu déjà mûr,
Chacun plantant, comme un outil, son bec impur
Dans tous les coins saignants de cette pourriture;

....

Or the eternal cooing of a dove! – Cythera was now nothing but the most meagre of lands, a rocky desert disturbed by sharp cries. I could half make out, however, a remarkable object!

It was not a temple set in bosky shades, where the young priestess, in love with the flowers, went forth, her body burning with secret heats, half-opening her robe to the passing breezes;

But, as we sailed near enough to the coast to disturb the birds with our white sails, we saw that it was a three-branched gibbet, standing out black against the sky, like a cypress.

Fierce birds perched on their food were furiously destroying a ripe, hanging corpse, each one planting his dirty beak, like an implement, in every bleeding corner of the rotten mass.

Les yeux étaient deux trous, et du ventre effondré
Les intestins pesants lui coulaient sur les cuisses,
Et ses bourreaux, gorgés de hideuses délices,
L'avaient à coups de bec absolument châtré.

Sous les pieds, un troupeau de jaloux quadrupèdes,
Le museau relevé, tournoyait et rôdait;
Une plus grande bête au milieu s'agitait
Comme un exécuteur entouré de ses aides.

Habitant de Cythère, enfant d'un ciel si beau,
Silencieusement tu souffrais ces insultes
En expiation de tes infâmes cultes
Et des péchés qui t'ont interdit le tombeau.

Ridicule pendu, tes douleurs sont les miennes!
Je sentis, à l'aspect de tes membres flottants,
Comme un vomissement, remonter vers mes dents
Le long fleuve de fiel des douleurs anciennes;

....

The eyes were two holes, and from the ruins of the belly the heavy
intestines were running down his thighs, and his torturers, gorged with
hideous titbits, had, with their beaks, completely castrated him.

Under the feet, a pack of greedy quadrupeds, their muzzles upturned,
were prowling around; one larger animal was busying itself in the middle,
like an executioner surrounded by his helpers.

Native of Cythera, born under such a beautiful sky, you were silently
suffering these insults, as an expiation of your infamous religious practices
and of the sins which denied you burial.

Laughable hanged man, your sufferings are my own! As I looked on your
formless limbs, I felt, rising towards my teeth like vomit, the long river of
gall of ancient sufferings.

Devant toi, pauvre diable au souvenir si cher,
J'ai senti tous les becs et toutes les mâchoires
Des corbeaux lancinants et des panthères noires
Qui jadis aimaient tant à triturer ma chair.

– Le ciel était charmant, la mer était unie;
Pour moi tout était noir et sanglant désormais,
Hélas! et j'avais, comme en un suaire épais,
Le cœur enseveli dans cette allégorie.

Dans ton île, ô Vénus! je n'ai trouvé debout
Qu'un gibet symbolique où pendait mon image . . .
– Ah! Seigneur! donnez-moi la force et le courage
De contempler mon cœur et mon corps sans dégoût!

....

Looking at you, poor wretch whose memory is so dear, I felt all the beaks and all the jaws of the tearing crows and the black panthers who once so loved to pulverize my flesh.

– The sky was delightful, the sea was smooth; for me now everything was black and bloody, alas! and I had, as if in a thick shroud, my heart buried in this allegory.

In your island, o Venus, I found nothing standing but a symbolic gibbet where my own image hung. O Lord! give me the strength and the courage to look on my heart and my body without disgust.

68 (CXVII) L'Amour et le Crâne

VIEUX CUL-DE-LAMPE

L'Amour est assis sur le crâne
        De l'Humanité,
Et sur ce trône le profane,
        Au rire effronté,

Souffle gaiement des bulles rondes
        Qui montent dans l'air,
Comme pour rejoindre les mondes
        Au fond de l'éther.

Le globe lumineux et frêle
        Prend un grand essor,
Crève et crache son âme grêle
        Comme un songe d'or.

J'entends le crâne à chaque bulle
        Prier et gémir:
— «Ce jeu féroce et ridicule,
        Quand doit-il finir?

....

Love and the Skull
AN OLD ENGRAVING

Cupid is sitting on the skull of Humanity, and on this throne the sinner, with his impudent laugh,

Is gaily blowing round bubbles, which rise into the air as if to reach the worlds at the far side of the ether.

The shining, fragile globe soars strongly, bursts and spits out its soul, slight as a golden dream.

I hear the skull, at each bubble, beg and cry in pain: 'This savage, ridiculous game — when will it end?

Car ce que ta bouche cruelle
    Eparpille en l'air,
Monstre assassin, c'est ma cervelle,
    Mon sang et ma chair!»

....

'For what your cruel mouth is scattering in the air, murderous monster, is my brain, my blood and my flesh!'

RÉVOLTE

(Revolt)

69 (CXVIII) Le Reniement de Saint Pierre

Qu'est-ce que Dieu fait donc de ce flot d'anathèmes
Qui monte tous les jours vers ses chers Séraphins?
Comme un tyran gorgé de viande et de vins,
Il s'endort au doux bruit de nos affreux blasphèmes.

Les sanglots des martyrs et des suppliciés
Sont une symphonie enivrante sans doute,
Puisque, malgré le sang que leur volupté coûte,
Les cieux ne s'en sont point encore rassasiés!

— Ah! Jésus, souviens-toi du Jardin des Olives!
Dans ta simplicité tu priais à genoux
Celui qui dans son ciel riait au bruit des clous
Que d'ignobles bourreaux plantaient dans tes chairs vives,

....

St Peter's Denial

Whatever does God do with the flood of anathemas that rises each day towards his dear Seraphim? Like a tyrant gorged with meat and wine he dozes off to the sweet sound of our dreadful blasphemies.

The sobs of the martyrs and the tortured are exhilarating music, no doubt, since despite the cost in blood of their pleasures the heavens have still not had their fill of them.

— Oh, Jesus, remember the Garden of Olives! In your simplicity you prayed on your knees to him who in his heaven laughed at the sounds of the nails that vile torturers were planting in your living flesh,

Lorsque tu vis cracher sur ta divinité
La crapule du corps de garde et des cuisines,
Et lorsque tu sentis s'enfoncer les épines
Dans ton crâne où vivait l'immense Humanité;

Quand de ton corps brisé la pesanteur horrible
Allongeait tes deux bras distendus, que ton sang
Et ta sueur coulaient de ton front pâlissant,
Quand tu fus devant tous posé comme une cible,

Rêvais-tu de ces jours si brillants et si beaux
Où tu vins pour remplir l'éternelle promesse,
Où tu foulais, monté sur une douce ânesse,
Des chemins tout jonchés de fleurs et de rameaux,

Où, le cœur tout gonflé d'espoir et de vaillance,
Tu fouettais tous ces vils marchands à tour de bras,
Où tu fus maître enfin? La remords n'a-t-il pas
Pénétré dans ton flanc plus avant que la lance?

— Certes, je sortirai, quant à moi, satisfait
D'un monde où l'action n'est pas la sœur du rêve;
Puissé-je user du glaive et périr par le glaive!
Saint Pierre a renié Jésus . . . il a bien fait!

....

When you saw them spit upon your divinity, the scum of the guardroom and the kitchens, and when you felt the thorns enter your skull, the dwelling-place of immense Humanity;

When the horrible weight of your broken body dragged upon your two dislocated arms, when your blood and your sweat ran down your paling forehead, when you were placed in front of everyone as a target,

Did you dream of those days, so brilliant and so beautiful, when you came to fulfil the eternal promise, when you walked, mounted on a gentle she-ass, over paths all strewn with flowers and branches?

When, your heart swollen with hope and bravery, you whipped those vile merchants with all your strength, when you were finally master? Did not remorse strike deeper into your side than the lance?

Certainly I, for my part, shall be glad to leave a world where action is not the sister of dreams. May I live by the sword and perish by the sword! St Peter denied Jesus . . . he was right.

70 (CXIX) Abel et Caïn

I

Race d'Abel, dors, bois et mange;
Dieu te sourit complaisamment.

Race de Caïn, dans la fange
Rampe et meurs misérablement.

Race d'Abel, ton sacrifice
Flatte le nez du Séraphin!

Race de Caïn, ton supplice
Aura-t-il jamais une fin?

Race d'Abel, vois tes semailles
Et ton bétail venir à bien;

Race de Caïn, tes entrailles
Hurlent la faim comme un vieux chien.

Race d'Abel, chauffe ton ventre
A ton foyer patriarcal;

....

Abel and Cain

I

Race of Abel, sleep, drink and eat; God smiles on you indulgently.
  Race of Cain, crawl in the mud, crawl and die in wretchedness.
  Race of Abel, your sacrifice is sweet in the nostrils of the Seraph!
  Race of Cain, will your torture ever end?
  Race of Abel, see your crops amd your cattle prosper;
  Race of Cain, your bowels are howling with hunger like an old dog.
  Race of Abel, warm your belly at your patriarch's hearth;

Race de Caïn, dans ton antre
Tremble de froid, pauvre chacal!

Race d'Abel, aime et pullule!
Ton or fait aussi des petits.

Race de Caïn, cœur qui brûle,
Prends garde à ces grands appétits.

Race d'Abel, tu croîs et broutes
Commes les punaises des bois!

Race de Caïn, sur les routes
Traîne ta famille aux abois.

II

Ah! race d'Abel, ta charogne
Engraissera le sol fumant!

Race de Caïn, ta besogne
N'est pas faite suffisamment;

Race d'Abel, voici ta honte:
Le fer est vaincu par l'épieu!

Race de Caïn, au ciel monte,
Et sur la terre jette Dieu!

....

Race of Cain, in your cave, shiver with cold, poor jackal.
Race of Abel, love and pullulate! Your gold, too, is breeding.
Race of Cain, burning heart, beware of those fierce appetites.
Race of Abel, you grow and feed like woodlice.
Race of Cain, along the roads, drag your desperate family.

II

Ah, race of Abel, your carcass will manure the steaming earth!
Race of Cain, you haven't finished the job;
Race of Abel, here is your shame: the sword is conquered by the hunting-spear!
Race of Cain, climb up to heaven and throw down God upon the earth!

71 (CXX) Les Litanies de Satan

O toi, le plus savant et le plus beau des Anges,
Dieu trahi par le sort et privé de louanges,

O Satan, prends pitié de ma longue misère!

O Prince de l'exil, à qui l'on a fait tort,
Et qui, vaincu, toujours te redresses plus fort,

O Satan, prends pitié de ma longue misère!

Toi qui sais tout, grande roi des choses souterraines,
Guérisseur familier des angoisses humaines,

O Satan, prends pitié de ma longue misère!

Toi qui, même aux lépreux, aux parias maudits,
Enseignes par l'amour le goût du Paradis,

O Satan, prends pitié de ma longue misère!

....

The Litanies of Satan

O most learned and beautiful of the Angels, a God betrayed by fate and
deprived of praises,
    O Satan, take pity on my long misery!
    O Prince of exile, to whom wrong was done, and who, vanquished, dost
always rise up in greater strength, o Satan . . .
    Thou who knowest all, great lord of the things which are under the earth,
familiar healer of human anguish, o Satan . . .
    Thou who even to the lepers, to the accursed outcasts, dost impart
through love the taste of Paradise, o Satan . . .

O toi qui de la Mort, ta vieille et forte amante,
Engendras l'Espérance, — une folle charmante!

O Satan, prends pitié de ma longue misère!

Toi qui fais au proscrit ce regard calme et haut
Qui damne tout un peuple autour d'un échafaud,

O Satan, prends pitié de ma longue misère!

Toi qui sais en quels coins des terres envieuses
Le Dieu jaloux cacha les pierres précieuses,

O Satan, prends pitié de ma longue misère!

Toi dont l'œil clair connaît les profonds arsenaux
Où dort enseveli le peuple des métaux,

O Satan, prends pitié de ma longue misère!

Toi dont la large main cache les précipices
Au somnambule errant au bord des édifices,

O Satan, prends pitié de ma longue misère!

Toi qui, magiquement, assouplis les vieux os
De l'ivrogne attardé foulé par les chevaux,

O Satan, prends pitié de ma longue misère!

....

O thou who upon Death, thy old and powerful mistress, didst beget
Hope, charming in her folly, o Satan . . .

Thou who givest to the condemned man that calm, lofty look that damns
a whole people gathered around a scaffold, o Satan . . .

Thou who knowest in what corners of envious earth a jealous God hid
precious stones, o Satan . . .

Thou whose clear eye knows the deep arsenals where the race of metals
lies sleeping, o Satan . . .

Thou whose broad hand hides the precipice from the sleepwalker wander-
ing at the edges of buildings, o Satan . . .

Thou who, magically, dost make supple the old bones of the late-walking
drunkard trampled by the horses, o Satan . . .

Toi qui, pour consoler l'homme frêle qui souffre,
Nous appris à mêler le salpêtre et le soufre,

O Satan, prends pitié de ma longue misère!

Toi qui poses ta marque, ô complice subtil,
Sur le front du Crésus impitoyable et vil,

O Satan, prends pitié de ma longue misère!

Toi qui mets dans les yeux et dans le cœur des filles
Le culte de la plaie et l'amour des guenilles,

O Satan, prends pitié de ma longue misère!

Bâton des exilés, lampe des inventeurs,
Confesseur des pendus et des conspirateurs,

O Satan, prends pitié de ma longue misère!

Père adoptif de ceux qu'en sa noire colère
Du paradis terrestre a chassés Dieu le Père,

O Satan, prends pitié de ma longue misère!

Thou who, to console frail man in his sufferings, hast taught us to mix saltpetre and sulphur, o Satan . . .

Thou who settest thy mark, o subtle accomplice, on the brow of the pitiless and vile Croesus, o Satan . . .

Thou who puttest in the eyes and the heart of girls the cult of wounds and the love of rags, o Satan . . .

Staff of exiles, lamp of inventors, confessor of gallow-birds and conspirators, o Satan . . .

Foster-father of those whom, in his black anger, God the Father expelled from the earthly paradise, o Satan . . .

PRIÈRE

Gloire et louange à toi, Satan, dans les hauteurs
Du Ciel, où tu régnas, et dans les profondeurs
De l'Enfer, où, vaincu, tu rêves en silence!
Fais que mon âme un jour, sous l'Arbre de Science,
Près de toi se repose, à l'heure où sur ton front
Comme un Temple nouveau ses rameaux s'épandront!

....

PRAYER

Glory and praise to thee, Satan, in the heights of Heaven, where thou didst
once reign, and in the depths of Hell where, vanquished, thou dreamest in
silence! Vouchsafe that my soul one day may rest in thee, under the Tree of
Knowledge, at the hour when over thy brow, like a new Temple, its
branches once more are spread.

LA MORT

(Death)

72 (CXXI) La Mort des Amants

Nous aurons des lits pleins d'odeurs légères,
Des divans profonds comme des tombeaux,
Et d'étranges fleurs sur des étagères,
Ecloses pour nous sous des cieux plus beaux.

Usant à l'envi leurs chaleurs dernières,
Nos deux cœurs seront deux vastes flambeaux,
Qui réfléchiront leurs doubles lumières
Dans nos deux esprits, ces miroirs jumeaux.

Un soir fait de rose et de bleu mystique,
Nous échangerons un éclair unique,
Comme un long sanglot, tout chargé d'adieux;

Et plus tard un Ange, entr'ouvrant les portes,
Viendra ranimer, fidèle et joyeux,
Les miroirs ternis et les flammes mortes.

....

The Death of Lovers

We shall have beds filled with light odours, couches deep as tombs, and, set
out on shelves, rare flowers which bloomed for us under more beautiful
skies.

    Vying to use up their last heats, our hearts will be two great torches,
which will reflect their double lights in our two spirits, those twin mirrors.

    One evening made of mystic blue and rose, we shall exchange a single
bolt of lightning, like a long sob, laden with farewells;

    And later an Angel, gently opening the doors, will come, faithful and
joyous, to revive the dulled mirrors and the dead flames.

73 (CXXII) La Mort des Pauvres

C'est la Mort qui console, hélas! et qui fait vivre;
C'est le but de la vie, et c'est le seul espoir
Qui, comme un élixir, nous monte et nous enivre,
Et nous donne le cœur de marcher jusqu'au soir;

A travers la tempête, et la neige, et le givre,
C'est la clarté vibrante à notre horizon noir;
C'est l'auberge fameuse inscrite sur le livre,
Où l'on pourra manger, et dormir, et s'asseoir;

C'est un Ange qui tient dans ses doigts magnétiques
Le sommeil et le don des rêves extatiques,
Et qui refait le lit des gens pauvres et nus;

C'est la gloire des dieux, c'est le grenier mystique,
C'est la bourse du pauvre et sa patrie antique,
C'est le portique ouvert sur les Cieux inconnus!

....

The Death of the Poor

It is Death which consoles men, alas, and keeps them alive. Death is the aim
of life; it is the only hope which, like an elixir, raises our spirits and
intoxicates us, and gives us the heart to march until evening;

Through the storm, and the snow, and the frost, it is the light pulsating
on our black horizon; it is the famous inn promised in the book where we
shall eat, and sleep, and sit down;

It is an Angel who holds in his magnetic fingers sleep and the gift of
ecstatic dreams, who makes up the bed of the poor and naked;

It is the glory of the gods, the mystic granary, the poor man's purse and
his ancient fatherland, it is the portico open on to the unknown Heavens!

74 (CXXIV) La Fin de la Journée

Sous une lumière blafarde
Court, danse et se tord sans raison
La Vie, impudente et criarde.
Aussi, sitôt qu'à l'horizon

La nuit voluptueuse monte,
Apaisant tout, même la faim,
Effaçant tout, même la honte,
Le Poète se dit: «Enfin!

Mon esprit, commes mes vertèbres,
Invoque ardemment le repos;
Le cœur plein de songes funèbres,

Je vais me coucher sur le dos
Et me rouler dans vos rideaux,
O rafraîchissantes ténèbres!»

....

The End of the Day

Under a bleak white light she runs, dances and writhes without reason –
Life, shameless and shrill. And so, as soon as on the horizon
   Voluptuous night rises, calming everything, even hunger, blotting out
everything, even shame, the Poet says to himself, 'At last!
   'My spirit, like my spine, ardently prays for rest; with a heart full of
funeral dreams,
   'I shall lie down on my back and roll myself up in your curtains, o
refreshing darkness!'

75 (CXXV) Le Rêve d'un Curieux

A F. N.

Connais-tu, comme moi, la douleur savoureuse,
Et de toi fais-tu dire: «Oh! l'homme singulier!»
– J'allais mourir. C'était dans mon âme amoureuse,
Désir mêlé d'horreur, un mal particulier;

Angoisse et vif espoir, sans humeur factieuse.
Plus allait se vidant le fatal sablier,
Plus ma torture était âpre et délicieuse;
Tout mon cœur s'arrachait au monde familier.

J'étais comme l'enfant avide du spectacle,
Haïssant le rideau comme on hait un obstacle . . .
Enfin la vérité froide se révéla:

J'étais mort sans surprise, et la terrible aurore
M'enveloppait. – Eh quoi! n'est-ce donc que cela?
La toile était levée et j'attendais encore.

....

The Dream of a Curious Man

Do you know, as I do, how suffering can be savoured, and do you make
people say of you, 'What a strange man!' I was going to die. My amorous
soul felt desire mingled with horror, an illness peculiar to itself;

Anguish and lively hope, without any impulse to protest. The lower the
fatal hourglass sank, the more savage and delicious was my torture; all my
heart was tearing itself away from the familiar world.

I was like the child desperate to see the play, hating the curtain as one
hates a barrier . . . At last the cold truth revealed itself:

I had died without surprise, and the terrible dawn was enfolding me. –
'What! Is that all?' The curtain had risen and I was still waiting.

76 (CXXVI) Le Voyage

A Maxime Du Camp

I

Pour l'enfant, amoureux de cartes et d'estampes,
L'univers est égal à son vaste appétit.
Ah! que le monde est grand à la clarté des lampes!
Aux yeux du souvenir que le monde est petit!

Un matin nous partons, le cerveau plein de flamme,
Le cœur gros de rancune et de désirs amers,
Et nous allons, suivant le rythme de la lame,
Berçant notre infini sur le fini des mers:

Les uns, joyeux de fuir une patrie infâme;
D'autres, l'horreur de leurs berceaux, et quelques-uns,
Astrologues noyés dans les yeux d'une femme,
La Circé tyrannique aux dangereux parfums.

....

The Voyage

I

For the child, in love with maps and prints, the universe is equal to his vast appetite. Oh, how big the world is by lamplight! In the eyes of memory, how small the world is!

One morning we leave, our brains full of fire, our hearts swollen with resentment and bitter desires, and we go, following the rhythm of the waves, rocking our infinity on the finitude of the seas:

Some of us happy to flee a dishonoured country; others, the horror of their cradles, and a few, astrologers drowned in the eyes of a woman, the tyranny of Circe and her dangerous perfumes.

Pour n'être pas changés en bêtes, ils s'enivrent
D'espace et de lumière et de cieux embrasés;
La glace qui les mord, les soleils qui les cuivrent,
Effacent lentement la marque des baisers.

Mais les vrais voyageurs sont ceux-là seuls qui partent
Pour partir; cœurs légers, semblables aux ballons,
De leur fatalité jamais ils ne s'écartent,
Et, sans savoir pourquoi, disent toujours: Allons!

Ceux-là dont les désirs ont la forme des nues,
Et qui rêvent, ainsi qu'un conscrit le canon,
De vastes voluptés, changeantes, inconnues,
Et dont l'esprit humain n'a jamais su le nom!

II

Nous imitons, horreur! la toupie et la boule
Dans leur valse et leurs bonds; même dans nos sommeils
La Curiosité nous tourmente et nous roule,
Comme un Ange cruel qui fouette des soleils.

....

So as not to be changed into animals, they drink deep of space and light and flaming skies; biting ice and burning suns slowly rub out the marks of kisses.

But the real travellers are those who leave for leaving's sake; their hearts are light as balloons, they never diverge from the path of their fate and, without knowing why, always say, 'Let's go.'

They are the ones whose desires have the shape of clouds, and who dream, as a new recruit dreams of cannon fire, of limitless pleasures, ever-changing, unknown, which the human mind has never been able to name.

II

We imitate, horror! the top and the ball in their waltzing and bouncing; even in our sleep Curiosity torments us and spins us about, like a cruel Angel whipping suns.

Singulière fortune où le but se déplace,
Et, n'étant nulle part, peut être n'importe où!
Où l'Homme, dont jamais l'espérance n'est lasse,
Pour trouver le repos court toujours comme un fou!

Notre âme est un trois-mâts cherchant son Icarie;
Une voix retentit sur le pont: «Ouvre l'œil!»
Une voix de la hune, ardente et folle, crie:
«Amour . . . gloire . . . bonheur!» Enfer! c'est un écueil!

Chaque îlot signalé par l'homme de vigie
Est un Eldorado promis par le Destin;
L'Imagination qui dresse son orgie
Ne trouve qu'un récif aux clartés du matin.

O le pauvre amoureux des pays chimériques!
Faut-il le mettre aux fers, le jeter à la mer,
Ce matelot ivrogne, inventeur d'Amériques
Dont le mirage rend le gouffre plus amer?

....

Strange fate whose objective is constantly moving and which, being
nowhere, can be anywhere! Where Man, whose hope never tires, seeks
repose by running for ever like a madman!

Our soul is a three-master searching for its Icaria. A voice calls out from
the bridge, 'Keep your eyes open!' From the crow's-nest a voice, ardent and
wild, cries, 'Love . . . glory . . . happiness!' Damnation! It's a rock.

Each islet spotted by the lookout is an Eldorado promised by Destiny;
Imagination, already setting up its orgy, finds only a reef in the light of
morning.

O the poor lover of chimerical countries! Shall we clap him in irons,
throw him over the side, that drunken sailor, discoverer of Americas whose
mirage makes the salt depths even more bitter?

Tel le vieux vagabond, piétinant dans la boue,
Rêve, le nez en l'air, de brillants paradis;
Son œil ensorcelé découvre une Capoue
Partout où la chandelle illumine un taudis.

III

Etonnants voyageurs! quelles nobles histoires
Nous lisons dans vos yeux profonds comme les mers!
Montrez-nous les écrins de vos riches mémoires,
Ces bijoux merveilleux, faits d'astres et d'éthers.

Nous voulons voyager sans vapeur et sans voile!
Faites, pour égayer l'ennui de nos prisons,
Passer sur nos esprits, tendus comme une toile,
Vos souvenirs avec leurs cadres d'horizons.

....

He is like the old vagabond shuffling in the mud and dreaming, with his nose in the air, of brilliant paradises; his bewitched eye discovers a Capua in each corner where the candle lights up a slum room.

III

Astonishing travellers! what noble tales we read in your eyes, deep as the seas! Show us the jewel-cases of your rich memories, those wonderful gems made of stars and ethers.

We want to travel without steam or sail! Won't you relieve the boredom of our imprisonment by projecting on our minds, stretched tight as a canvas, your memories in their settings of horizons?

Dites, qu'avez-vous vu?

IV

«Nous avons vu des astres
Et des flots; nous avons vu des sables aussi;
Et, malgré bien des chocs et d'imprévus désastres,
Nous nous sommes souvent ennuyés, comme ici.

La gloire du soleil sur la mer violette,
La gloire des cités dans le soleil couchant,
Allumaient dans nos cœurs une ardeur inquiète
De plonger dans un ciel au reflet alléchant.

Les plus riches cités, les plus grands paysages,
Jamais ne contenaient l'attrait mystérieux
De ceux que le hasard fait avec les nuages.
Et toujours le désir nous rendait soucieux!

– La jouissance ajoute au désir de la force.
Désir, vieil arbre à qui le plaisir sert d'engrais,
Cependant que grossit et durcit ton écorce,
Tes branches veulent voir le soleil de plus près!

....

Tell us, what did you see?

IV

'We saw stars and waves; we saw sands too; and,
in spite of many shocks and unexpected disasters, we were often bored, there
as here.

'The glory of the sun on the violet sea, the glory of cities in the setting
sun, sparked off in our hearts a restless desire to plunge into a sky with
alluring reflections.

'The richest cities, the broadest landscapes, never held the mysterious
attraction of those which chance makes out of the clouds. And desire always
made us uneasy!

'– Enjoyment adds strength to desire. Desire, old tree that pleasure
manures, as your bark thickens and hardens, your branches want to see the
sun nearer at hand.

Grandiras-tu toujours, grand arbre plus vivace
Que le cyprès? – Pourtant nous avons, avec soin,
Cueilli quelques croquis pour votre album vorace,
Frères qui trouvez beau tout ce qui vient de loin!

Nous avons salué des idoles à trompe;
Des trônes constellés de joyaux lumineux;
Des palais ouvragés dont la féerique pompe
Serait pour vos banquiers un rêve ruineux;

Des costumes qui sont pour les yeux une ivresse;
Des femmes dont les dents et les ongles sont teints,
Et des jongleurs savants que le serpent caresse.»

V

Et puis, et puis encore?

VI

«O cerveaux enfantins!

....

'Will you always go on growing, great tree hardier than the cypress? –
And yet we did, carefully, make some sketches for your insatiable album,
dear brothers who think anything is beautiful that has come from far away!

'We saluted idols with elephants' trunks; thrones studded with shining
jewels; fine-wrought palaces whose faery splendour would be a ruinous
dream for your bankers;

'Costumes that are an intoxication for the eyes; women whose teeth and
nails are dyed, and knowing jugglers whom serpents caress.'

V
And then, and then? What then?

VI
                          'O childish brains!

Pour ne pas oublier la chose capitale,
Nous avons vu partout, et sans l'avoir cherché,
Du haut jusques en bas de l'échelle fatale,
Le spectacle ennuyeux de l'immortel péché:

La femme, esclave vile, orgueilleuse et stupide,
Sans rire s'adorant et s'aimant sans dégoût;
L'homme, tyran goulu, paillard, dur et cupide,
Esclave de l'esclave et ruisseau dans l'égout;

Le bourreau qui jouit, le martyr qui sanglote;
La fête qu'assaisonne et parfume le sang;
Le poison du pouvoir énervant le despote,
Et le peuple amoureux du fouet abrutissant;

Plusieurs religions semblables à la nôtre,
Toutes escaladant le ciel; la Sainteté,
Comme en un lit de plume un délicat se vautre,
Dans les clous et le crin cherchant la volupté;

'Not to forget the most important thing, we saw everywhere, and without having to look for it, from the top to the bottom of the ladder of existence, the tedious spectacle of immortal sin:

'Woman, a slave, contemptible, proud and stupid, adoring herself without laughing and loving herself without disgust; man, a greedy tyrant, lecherous, hard and covetous, slave to the slave and a gutter in the sewer;

'The executioner relishing his task, the sobbing martyr, the festival seasoned and perfumed with blood; the poison of power unmanning the despot and the people in love with the stultifying whip.

'Several religions similar to ours, all taking heaven by storm; Sainthood, like a voluptuary wallowing in a feather-bed, seeking its pleasure among nails and horsehair.

L'Humanité bavarde, ivre de son génie,
Et, folle maintenant comme elle était jadis,
Criant à Dieu, dans sa furibonde agonie:
'O mon semblable, ô mon maître, je te maudis!'

Et les moins sots, hardis amants de la Démence,
Fuyant le grand troupeau parqué par le Destin,
Et se réfugiant dans l'opium immense!
– Tel est du globe entier l'éternel bulletin.»

VII

Amer savoir, celui qu'on tire du voyage!
Le monde, monotone et petit, aujourd'hui,
Hier, demain, toujours, nous fait voir notre image:
Une oasis d'horreur dans un désert d'ennui!

Faut-il partir? rester? Si tu peux rester, reste;
Pars, s'il le faut. L'un court, et l'autre se tapit
Pour tromper l'ennemi vigilant et funeste,
Le Temps! Il est, hélas! des coureurs sans répit,

....

'Chattering Humanity, intoxicated with its own genius and mad now as
ever, shouting at God, in its furious death agony, "O my equal, o my
master, I curse you!"

'And the less stupid, the bold lovers of Dementia, fleeing from the great
herd penned by Destiny, and taking refuge in immense opium! – That is the
eternal news from the entire globe.'

VII

It is bitter knowledge that comes from travelling! The world, monotonous
and small, today, yesterday, tomorrow, always, shows us our own image: an
oasis of horror in a desert of tedium!

Should we leave? Stay? If you can stay, stay; leave, if you must. One man
runs, another cowers to deceive the vigilant, deadly enemy, Time! There
are, alas, tireless runners,

Comme le Juif errant et comme les apôtres,
A qui rien ne suffit, ni wagon ni vaisseau,
Pour fuir ce rétiaire infâme; il en est d'autres
Qui savent le tuer sans quitter leur berceau.

Lorsque enfin il mettra le pied sur notre échine,
Nous pourrons espérer et crier: En avant!
De même qu'autrefois nous partions pour la Chine,
Les yeux fixés au large et les cheveux au vent,

Nous nous embarquerons sur la mer des Ténèbres
Avec le cœur joyeux d'un jeune passager.
Entendez-vous ces voix, charmantes et funèbres,
Qui chantent: «Par ici! vous qui voulez manger

Le Lotus parfumé! c'est ici qu'on vendange
Les fruits miraculeux dont votre cœur a faim;
Venez vous enivrer de la douceur étrange
De cette après-midi qui n'a jamais de fin»?

....

Like the Wandering Jew and the apostles, whom nothing, no wagon, no ship will serve to flee his dreadful net; there are others who manage to kill him without leaving their cradles.

When he finally puts his foot down on our necks, we will be able to hope and cry 'Forward!' Just as we once left for China with our eyes fixed on the open sea and our hair in the wind,

We shall set sail upon the Sea of Darkness with the joyful heart of a young passenger. Do you hear those voices, charming and deathly? They sing, 'This way, you who want to eat

Of the scented Lotus! This is where men gather the wondrous fruits that your heart desires; come and be lost in the strange sweetness of this afternoon that has no end.'

A l'accent familier nous devinons le spectre;
Nos Pylades là-bas tendent leurs bras vers nous.
«Pour rafraîchir ton cœur nage vers ton Electre!»
Dit celle dont jadis nous baisions les genoux.

VIII

O Mort, vieux capitaine, il est temps! levons l'ancre!
Ce pays nous ennuie, ô Mort! Appareillons!
Si le ciel et la mer sont noirs comme de l'encre,
Nos cœurs que tu connais sont remplis de rayons!

Verse-nous ton poison pour qu'il nous réconforte!
Nous voulons, tant ce feu nous brûle le cerveau,
Plonger au fond du gouffre, Enfer ou Ciel, qu'importe?
Au fond de l'Inconnu pour trouver du *nouveau!*

....

The familiar accents let us recognize the ghost; our dear friends are there,
holding out their arms to us. 'To refresh your heart, swim towards your
Electra!' says she whose knees we used once to kiss.

VIII

O Death, old captain, it is time! Let us weigh anchor! This country is tedious
to us, o Death! Let us make ready! If the sky and the sea are as black as ink,
our hearts which you know are full of rays of light.

Pour us your poison and let it strengthen us! We want, such is the fire that
burns our brains, to plunge into the depths of the abyss, Hell or Heaven,
what does it matter? To the depths of the unknown to find something *new*.

LES ÉPAVES

(From the Wreck)

LES ÉPAVES

(From the Wreck)

77 (v) A Celle qui est Trop Gaie

Ta tête, ton geste, ton air
Sont beaux comme un beau paysage;
Le rire joue en ton visage
Comme un vent frais dans un ciel clair.

Le passant chagrin que tu frôles
Est ébloui par la santé
Qui jaillit comme une clarté
De tes bras et de tes épaules.

Les retentissantes couleurs
Dont tu parsèmes tes toilettes
Jettent dans l'esprit des poètes
L'image d'un ballet de fleurs.

....

To a Woman who is Too Gay

Your head, your gestures, your look are as beautiful as a beautiful landscape; laughter plays on your face like a cool breeze in a clear sky.

The ill-tempered man whom you brush in passing is dazzled by the health which springs forth like a brightness from your arms and your shoulders.

The striking colours with which you scatter your outfits sow in the mind of poets the image of a ballet of flowers.

Ces robes folles sont l'emblème
De ton esprit bariolé;
Folle dont je suis affolé,
Je te hais autant que je t'aime!

Quelquefois dans un beau jardin
Où je traînais mon atonie,
J'ai senti, comme une ironie,
Le soleil déchirer mon sein;

Et le printemps et la verdure
Ont tant humilié mon cœur,
Que j'ai puni sur une fleur
L'insolence de la Nature.

Ainsi je voudrais, une nuit,
Quand l'heure des voluptés sonne,
Vers les trésors de ta personne,
Comme un lâche, ramper sans bruit,

Pour châtier ta chair joyeuse,
Pour meurtrir ton sein pardonné,
Et faire à ton flanc étonné
Une blessure large et creuse,

....

Those crazy dresses are the emblem of your variegated spirit; madwoman,
I am mad about you, I hate you as much as I love you.

Sometimes in a beautiful garden where I was dragging my lethargy
along, I have felt, as if it were an irony, the sun tearing my breast open,

And the spring and the green leaves have so humiliated my heart that I
have punished upon a flower the insolence of Nature.

So I would wish, one night, when the hour of pleasure strikes, to
approach the treasures of your person, like a coward, creeping noiselessly,

And there to punish your joyous flesh, to bruise your ransomed breast,
and make in your surprised loins a large, hollow wound,

Et, vertigineuse douceur!
A travers ces lèvres nouvelles,
Plus éclatantes et plus belles,
T'infuser mon venin, ma sœur!

78 (VI) Les Bijoux

La très chère était nue, et, connaissant mon cœur,
Elle n'avait gardé que ses bijoux sonores,
Dont le riche attirail lui donnait l'air vainqueur
Qu'ont dans leurs jours heureux les esclaves des Mores.

Quand il jette en dansant son bruit vif et moqueur,
Ce monde rayonnant de métal et de pierre
Me ravit en extase, et j'aime à la fureur
Les choses où le son se mêle à la lumière.

Elle était donc couchée et se laissait aimer,
Et du haut du divan elle souriait d'aise
A mon amour profond et doux comme la mer,
Qui vers elle montait comme vers sa falaise.

....

And, dizzying sweetness!, through these new lips, more dazzling and more beautiful, to pour my venom into you, sister!

The Jewels

My darling was naked, and, knowing my heart, she had kept on only her sounding jewels, whose rich array gave her the all-conquering look that the slaves of the Moors have in their happier times.

When, as it moves, it throws out its sharp, mocking sound, that glittering world of metal and stone ravishes me into ecstasy, and I love to distraction things where sound is mingled with light.

She was lying there, then, and letting herself be loved, and from her vantage point on the couch she smiled happily at my love, deep and gentle as the sea, as it rose towards her as if to its cliff.

Les yeux fixés sur moi, comme un tigre dompté,
D'un air vague et rêveur elle essayait des poses,
Et la candeur unie à la lubricité
Donnait un charme neuf à ses métamorphoses;

Et son bras et sa jambe, et sa cuisse et ses reins,
Polis comme de l'huile, onduleux comme un cygne,
Passaient devant mes yeux clairvoyants et sereins;
Et son ventre et ses seins, ces grappes de ma vigne,

S'avançaient, plus câlins que les Anges du mal,
Pour troubler le repos où mon âme était mise,
Et pour la déranger du rocher de cristal
Où, calme et solitaire, elle s'était assise.

Je croyais voir unis par un nouveau dessin
Les hanches de l'Antiope au buste d'un imberbe,
Tant sa taille faisait ressortir son bassin.
Sur ce teint fauve et brun, le fard était superbe!

....

Her eyes fixed on me like a tamed tiger's, with a dreamy, vague look she
tried out new poses, and the combination of candour and lubricity lent a
new charm to her various shapes;

And her arm and her leg, and her thigh and her hips, smooth as oil,
undulating like a swan, passed before my eyes, all-seeing and serene; and her
belly and her breasts, those clusters of my vine,

Thrust forward, more tempting than the Angels of evil, to trouble the
state of rest my soul had entered, and to displace it from the crystal rock
where, calm and alone, it had seated itself.

I felt I was seeing, by some new device, the haunches of Antiope joined to
the torso of a beardless youth, so strongly did her waist set off her pelvis. On
that wild, brown skin the make-up was wonderful!

– Et la lampe s'étant résignée à mourir,
Comme le foyer seul illuminait la chambre,
Chaque fois qu'il poussait un flamboyant soupir,
Il inondait de sang cette peau couleur d'ambre!

....

– And the lamp having died down at last, as the fire alone lit up the chamber, every time it heaved a flaming sigh, it flooded with blood that amber-coloured skin.

GALANTERIES

(*Poetic Compliments*)

79 (VIII) Le Jet d'Eau

Tes beaux yeux sont las, pauvre amante!
Reste longtemps, sans les rouvrir,
Dans cette pose nonchalante
Où t'a surprise le plaisir.
Dans la cour le jet d'eau qui jase
Et ne se tait ni nuit ni jour,
Entretient doucement l'extase
Où ce soir m'a plongé l'amour.

> La gerbe épanouie
>   En mille fleurs,
> Où Phœbé réjouie
>   Met ses couleurs,
> Tombe comme une pluie
>   De larges pleurs.

....

The Fountain

Your beautiful eyes are tired, poor lover! Stay a long time, without opening them again, in that careless pose in which pleasure caught you. In the courtyard the fountain, babbling and never silent by night or day, gently prolongs the ecstasy into which love has plunged me this evening.

The spray, spreading into a thousand flowers, where joyous Phoebe puts her colours, falls like a rain of ample tears.

Ainsi ton âme qu'incendie
L'éclair brûlant des voluptés
S'élance, rapide et hardie,
Vers les vastes cieux enchantés.
Puis, elle s'épanche, mourante,
En un flot de triste langueur,
Qui par une invisible pente
Descend jusqu'au fond de mon cœur.

> La gerbe épanouie
>   En mille fleurs,
> Où Phœbé réjouie
>   Met ses couleurs,
> Tombe comme une pluie
>   De larges pleurs.

O toi, que la nuit rend si belle,
Qu'il m'est doux, penché vers tes seins,
D'écouter la plainte éternelle
Qui sanglote dans les bassins!
Lune, eau sonore, nuit bénie,
Arbres qui frissonnez autour,
Votre pure mélancolie
Est le miroir de mon amour.

....

Thus your soul, set on fire by the blazing flash of pleasure, springs up,
rapid and bold, towards the great enchanted skies. Then, dying, it spills over
in a flood of sad languor, which, by an invisible slope, runs down into the
depths of my heart.
The spray . . .
O you, whom night makes so beautiful, how sweet it is to me, leaning
towards your breasts, to listen to the eternal plaint which sobs in the pools.
Moon, sounding water, blessed night, trees shivering around us, your pure
melancholy is the mirror of my love.

La gerbe épanouie
En mille fleurs,
Où Phœbé réjouie
Met ses couleurs,
Tombe comme une pluie
De larges pleurs.

80 (x) Hymne

A la très chère, à la très belle
Qui remplit mon cœur de clarté,
A l'ange, à l'idole immortelle,
Salut en l'immortalité!

Elle se répand dans ma vie
Comme un air imprégné de sel,
Et dans mon âme inassouvie
Verse le goût de l'éternel.

Sachet toujours frais qui parfume
L'atmosphère d'un cher réduit,
Encensoir oublié qui fume
En secret à travers la nuit,

....

The spray . . .

Hymn

To the dearest one, to the fairest one, who fills my heart with light, to the angel, to the immortal idol, hail in immortality!

She permeates my life like an air impregnated with salt and into my unsatisfied soul she pours the taste of eternal things.

Unfading sachet that perfumes the atmosphere of a dear retreat, forgotten censer that smokes secretly throughout the night,

Comment, amour incorruptible,
T'exprimer avec vérité?
Grain de musc qui gis, invisible,
Au fond de mon éternité!

A la très bonne, à la très belle,
Qui fait ma joie et ma santé,
A l'ange, à l'idole immortelle,
Salut en l'immortalité!

....

How, o incorruptible love, can I express you truthfully? Grain of musk, you who lie invisible at the heart of my eternity!

To the best, the fairest one, who is all my joy and my health, to the angel, the immortal idol, hail in immortality!

81 (XII) Le Monstre

OU LE PARANYMPHE D'UNE NYMPHE MACABRE

I

Tu n'es certes pas, ma très chère,
Ce que Veuillot nomme un tendron.
Le jeu, l'amour, la bonne chère,
Bouillonnent en toi, vieux chaudron!
Tu n'es plus fraîche, ma très chère,

Ma vieille infante! Et cependant
Tes caravanes insensées
T'ont donné ce lustre abondant
Des choses qui sont très usées,
Mais qui séduisent cependant.

Je ne trouve pas monotone
La verdeur de tes quarante ans;
Je préfère tes fruits, Automne,
Aux fleurs banales du Printemps!
Non, tu n'es jamais monotone!

....

The Monster

OR THE SATIRICAL EULOGY OF A MACABRE NYMPH

I

You are certainly not, my dearest, what Veuillot would call a sprig of youth. Gambling, love, good living are boiling away inside you, old cauldron! You are no longer fresh, my dearest,

My old infanta! And yet, your crazy escapades have given you that deep patina of things which are heavily worn but attractive nevertheless.

I don't find it boring, the vigour of your forty years; I prefer your fruits, Autumn, to the commonplace flowers of Spring! No, you are never boring!

Ta carcasse a des agréments
Et des grâces particulières;
Je trouve d'étranges piments
Dans le creux de tes deux salières;
Ta carcasse a des agréments!

Nargue des amants ridicules
Du melon et du giraumont!
Je préfère tes clavicules
A celles du roi Salomon,
Et je plains ces gens ridicules!

Tes cheveux, comme un casque bleu,
Ombragent ton front de guerrière,
Qui ne pense et rougit que peu,
Et puis se sauvent par derrière
Comme les crins d'un casque bleu.

Tes yeux qui semblent de la boue,
Où scintille quelque fanal,
Ravivés au fard de ta joue,
Lancent un éclair infernal!
Tes yeux sont noirs comme la boue!

....

Your carcass has attractions and graces all its own; I find strange spice in
the hollows of your two salt-cellars. Your carcass has certain attractions!

To hell with the ridiculous lovers of melons and fat gourds! I prefer your
clavicles to King Solomon's, and I feel sorry for those ridiculous people.

Your hair, like a blue helmet, hangs over your warrior's brow, which
thinks little and blushes less, and then it flies away backwards like the crest
of a blue helmet.

Your eyes which look like mud amid which some beacon sparkles,
brightened by the rouge on your cheeks, flash out a devilish lightning. Your
eyes are black as mud!

Par sa luxure et son dédain
Ta lèvre amère nous provoque;
Cette lèvre, c'est un Eden
Qui nous attire et qui nous choque.
Quelle luxure! et quel dédain!

Ta jambe musculeuse et sèche
Sait gravir au haut des volcans,
Et malgré la neige et la dèche
Danser les plus fougueux cancans.
Ta jambe est musculeuse et sèche;

Ta peau brûlante et sans douceur,
Comme celle des vieux gendarmes,
Ne connaît pas plus la sueur
Que ton œil ne connaît les larmes.
(Et pourtant elle a sa douceur!)

II

Sotte, tu t'en vas droit au Diable!
Volontiers j'irais avec toi,
Si cette vitesse effroyable
Ne me causait pas quelque émoi.
Va-t'en donc, toute seule, au Diable!

By its lust and disdain your bitter lip excites us; that lip is an Eden that attracts and that shocks us. What lust! And what disdain!

Your muscular, thin leg can climb to the top of volcanoes, and in spite of snow and empty pockets can dance the wildest cancans. Your leg is muscular and thin.

Your burning, rough skin, no softer than that of old soldiers, no more knows sweat than your eye knows tears (and yet it has its own sweetness!).

II

Fool, you're going straight to the Devil! And I'd happily go with you, if the terrible speed wasn't a trifle upsetting. Go on then, by yourself, to the Devil!

Mon rein, mon poumon, mon jarret
Ne me laissent plus rendre hommage
A ce Seigneur, comme il faudrait.
«Hélas! c'est vraiment bien dommage!»
Disent mon rein et mon jarret.

Oh! très sincèrement je souffre
De ne pas aller aux sabbats,
Pour voir, quand il pète du soufre,
Comment tu lui baises son cas!
Oh! très sincèrement je souffre!

Je suis diablement affligé
De ne pas être ta torchère,
Et de te demander congé,
Flambeau d'enfer! Juge, ma chère,
Combien je dois être affligé,

Puisque depuis longtemps je t'aime,
Etant très logique! En effet,
Voulant du Mal chercher la crème
Et n'aimer qu'un monstre parfait,
Vraiment oui! vieux monstre, je t'aime!

....

My back, my lungs, my hamstrings no longer allow me to pay homage
to that Lord as I should. 'Alas! It really is a pity!' say my back and my legs.

I really am sincerely sorry not to be able to go to sabbaths, to see him
farting sulphur and you kissing his you-know-what. Oh, I'm so very sorry!

I'm devilishly upset not to be your candlestick, and to excuse myself, light
of hell! Imagine, my dear, how upset I must be,

Since I have long loved you, being the logical type! For, as I have been
trying to find the cream of Evil and to love only a perfect monster, it must
follow, my old monster – I love you.

PIÈCES DIVERSES

(*Various Pieces*)

82 (XVIII) L'Imprévu

Harpagon, qui veillait son père agonisant,
Se dit, rêveur, devant ces lèvres déjà blanches:
«Nous avons au grenier un nombre suffisant,
      Ce me semble, de vieilles planches?»

Célimène roucoule et dit: «Mon cœur est bon,
Et naturellement, Dieu m'a faite très belle.»
– Son cœur! cœur racorni, fumé comme un jambon,
      Recuit à la flamme éternelle!

Un gazetier fumeux, qui se croit un flambeau,
Dit au pauvre, qu'il a noyé dans les ténèbres:
«Où donc l'aperçois-tu, ce créateur du Beau,
      Ce Redresseur que tu célèbres?»

....

The Unforeseen

Harpagon, watching over his dying father, said dreamily, looking at those whitening lips, 'I *think* we have the right number of old planks in the attic . . .'

Celimene coos and says, 'I'm kind-hearted, and of course the Lord made me very beautiful.' Kind-hearted! A heart of leather, smoked like a ham, twice cooked in the eternal flame.

An addle-brained hack who thinks himself a shining light says to the poor man whom he has sunk in darkness, 'Where do you see him then, this creator of the Beautiful, this Righter of Wrongs whom you celebrate?'

Mieux que tous, je connais certain voluptueux
Qui bâille nuit et jour, et se lamente et pleure,
Répétant, l'impuissant et le fat: «Oui, je veux
    Etre vertueux, dans une heure!»

L'horloge, à son tour, dit à voix basse: «Il est mûr,
Le damné! J'avertis en vain la chair infecte.
L'homme est aveugle, sourd, fragile, comme un mur
    Qu'habite et que ronge un insecte!»

Et puis, Quelqu'un paraît, que tous avaient nié,
Et qui leur dit, railleur et fier: «Dans mon ciboire,
Vous avez, que je crois, assez communié,
    A la joyeuse Messe noire?

Chacun de vous m'a fait un temple dans son cœur;
Vous avez, en secret, baisé ma fesse immonde!
Reconnaissez Satan à son rire vainqueur,
    Enorme et laid comme le monde!

....

  Best of all, I know a certain voluptuary who yawns night and day, and
weeps and wails, repeating, the impotent boaster, 'Yes, I do want to be
virtuous – an hour from now.'

  The clock in its turn says in a low voice, 'He is ready for damnation! I
warn his diseased flesh, but in vain. Man is blind, deaf, frail as a wall infested
and gnawed by an insect.'

  And then Someone appears whom they had all denied, and who says to
them, mocking and proud, 'From my ciborium, I think, you all took
communion often enough at our happy Black Masses.

  'Each of you made me a temple in his heart; in secret, you kissed my
filthy buttocks! Now recognize Satan by his victorious laugh, huge and ugly
as the world itself.'

Avez-vous donc pu croire, hypocrites surpris,
Qu'on se moque du maître, et qu'avec lui l'on triche,
Et qu'il soit naturel de recevoir deux prix,
        D'aller au Ciel et d'être riche?

Il faut que le gibier paye le vieux chasseur
Qui se morfond longtemps à l'affût de la proie.
Je vais vous emporter à travers l'épaisseur,
        Compagnons de ma triste joie,

A travers l'épaisseur de la terre et du roc,
A travers les amas confus de votre cendre,
Dans un palais aussi grand que moi, d'un seul bloc,
        Et qui n'est pas de pierre tendre;

Car il est fait avec l'universel Péché,
Et contient mon orgueil, ma douleur et ma gloire!»
– Cependant, tout en haut de l'univers juché,
        Un Ange sonne la victoire

'Did you really think, you wide-eyed hypocrites, that you could mock the master and play games with him, and that it's natural to win two prizes, to go to Heaven and to be rich?

'The catch must reward the old hunter who has been long a-freezing, lying in wait for his prey. I am going to take you away through the thickness of matter, companions of my gloomy joys;

'Through the thickness of earth and rock, through the jumbled heaps of your ashes, to a palace as large as myself, made of a single block, and which is not of soft stone;

'For it is made of universal Sin, and contains my pride, my sorrow and my glory!' – Meanwhile, perched on the topmost point of the universe, an angel sounds the victory

De ceux dont le cœur dit: «Que béni soit ton fouet,
Seigneur! que la douleur, ô Père, soit bénie!
Mon âme dans tes mains n'est pas un vain jouet,
        Et ta prudence est infinie.»

Le son de la trompette est si délicieux,
Dans ces soirs solennels de célestes vendanges,
Qu'il s'infiltre comme une extase dans tous ceux
        Dont elle chante les louanges.

83 (XIX) La Rançon

L'homme a, pour payer sa rançon,
Deux champs au tuf profond et riche,
Qu'il faut qu'il remue et défriche
Avec le fer de la raison;

Pour obtenir la moindre rose,
Pour extorquer quelques épis,
Des pleurs salés de son front gris
Sans cesse il faut qu'il les arrose.

....

Of those whose heart says, 'Blessed be thy scourge, o Lord! blessed be
suffering, o Father! My soul is not an idle toy in thy hands, and thy
wisdom is infinite!'

The sound of the trumpet is so delectable, on those evenings of heavenly
harvest, that it filters like an ecstasy into all those whose praises it sings.

The Ransom

Man has, to pay his ransom, two fields of rich, deep soil, which he must dig
and clear with the spade of reason.

To see the smallest rose, to wrest a few ears of corn from them, he must
ceaselessly water them with the salt tears of his grey brow.

L'un est l'Art, et l'autre l'Amour.
– Pour rendre le juge propice,
Lorsque de la stricte justice
Paraîtra le terrible jour,

Il faudra lui montrer des granges
Pleines de moissons, et des fleurs
Dont les formes et les couleurs
Gagnent le suffrage des Anges.

....

One is Art, the other is Love. To have the judge on his side, when the terrible day of justice dawns,

He will have to show barns full of harvests, and flowers whose shapes and colours will win the vote of the Angels.

POEMS ADDED IN 1868

84 Epigraphe pour un Livre Condamné

Lecteur paisible et bucolique,
Sobre et naïf homme de bien,
Jette ce livre saturnien,
Orgiaque et mélancolique.

Si tu n'as fait ta rhétorique
Chez Satan, le rusé doyen,
Jette! tu n'y comprendrais rien,
Ou tu me croirais hystérique.

Mais si, sans se laisser charmer,
Ton œil sait plonger dans les gouffres,
Lis-moi, pour apprendre à m'aimer;

Ame curieuse qui souffres
Et vas cherchant ton paradis,
Plains-moi! . . . Sinon, je te maudis!

....

Epigraph for a Condemned Book

Peaceful, bucolic reader, temperate, artless and good-living, throw away this
saturnine, orgiastic and melancholy book.

Unless you've finished the rhetoric course at Satan's school, that wily
professor, throw it away! You wouldn't understand anything in it, or you would
say I was hysterical.

But if, without letting yourself be drawn in, your eye can look down into
abysses, read me, and learn to love me;

Curious, suffering soul, travelling in search of paradise, pity me! . . . Or
else I will curse you.

85 Madrigal Triste

I

Que m'importe que tu sois sage?
Sois belle! et sois triste! Les pleurs
Ajoutent un charme au visage,
Comme le fleuve au paysage;
L'orage rajeunit les fleurs.

Je t'aime surtout quand la joie
S'enfuit de ton front terrassé;
Quand ton cœur dans l'horreur se noie;
Quand sur ton présent se déploie
Le nuage affreux du passé.

Je t'aime quand ton grand œil verse
Une eau chaude comme le sang;
Quand, malgré ma main qui te berce,
Ton angoisse, trop lourde, perce
Comme un râle d'agonisant.

....

Sad Madrigal

I

What do I care if you are good? Be beautiful! And be sad! Tears add charm
to a face as a river does to the landscape; the storm revives the flowers.

I love you above all when joy flees from your prostrate brow; when your
heart is drowning in horror; when over your present there spreads the
hideous cloud of the past.

I love you when your great eye pours out water hot as blood; when, in
spite of my hand rocking you, your anguish, too heavy to bear, breaks
through like a death-rattle.

J'aspire, volupté divine!
Hymne profond, délicieux!
Tous les sanglots de ta poitrine,
Et crois que ton cœur s'illumine
Des perles que versent tes yeux!

II

Je sais que ton cœur, qui regorge
De vieux amours déracinés,
Flamboie encor comme une forge,
Et que tu couves sous ta gorge
Un peu de l'orgueil des damnés;

Mais tant, ma chère, que tes rêves
N'auront pas reflété l'Enfer,
Et qu'en un cauchemar sans trêves,
Songeant de poisons et de glaives,
Eprise de poudre et de fer,

....

I inhale – godlike pleasure! deep, delicious hymn! – all the sobs of your bosom, and I believe that your heart is lit up by the pearls that fall from your eyes.

II

I know that your heart, which overflows with old, uprooted loves, still blazes like a forge, and that you hide away under your breasts some of the pride of the damned;

But so long, my dear, as your dreams have not reflected Hell, and until, caught in a relentless nightmare, dreaming of poison and blades, in love with gunpowder and iron,

N'ouvrant à chacun qu'avec crainte,
Déchiffrant le malheur partout,
Te convulsant quand l'heure tinte,
Tu n'auras pas senti l'étreinte
De l'irrésistible Dégoût,

Tu ne pourras, esclave reine
Qui ne m'aimes qu'avec effroi,
Dans l'horreur de la nuit malsaine
Me dire, l'âme de cris pleine:
«Je suis ton égale, ô mon Roi!»

....

Opening your door only in fear, seeing signs of calamity everywhere, starting when the hour strikes, you have felt the grip of irresistible Disgust,

You will not, slave-queen, who loves me only in fear and trembling, be able, in the horror of the morbid night, to say to me, your soul filled with cries, 'I am your equal, o my King!'

86 La Prière d'un Païen

Ah! ne ralentis pas tes flammes;
Réchauffe mon cœur engourdi,
Volupté, torture des âmes!
Diva! supplicem exaudi!

Déesse dans l'air répandue,
Flamme dans notre souterrain!
Exauce une âme morfondue,
Qui te consacre un chant d'airain.

Volupté, sois toujours ma reine!
Prends le masque d'une sirène
Faite de chair et de velours,

Ou verse-moi tes sommeils lourds
Dans le vin informe et mystique,
Volupté, fantôme élastique!

....

The Pagan's Prayer

Ah, do not slow your flames; heat up my sluggish heart, Pleasure, torture of souls! *Diva! supplicem exaudi!*

Goddess at large in the air, flame of our subterranean depths, hear a soul dying of cold, who lifts up towards you a song of bronze.

Pleasure, be ever my queen! Put on the mask of a siren made of flesh and velvet,

Or pour out for me your heavy slumbers in formless, mystical wine, Pleasure, shape-changing phantom!

87 Le Rebelle

Un Ange furieux fond du ciel comme un aigle,
Du mécréant saisit à plein poing les cheveux,
Et dit, le secouant: «Tu connaîtras la règle!
(Car je suis ton bon Ange, entends-tu?) Je le veux!

Sache qu'il faut aimer, sans faire la grimace,
La pauvre, le méchant, le tortu, l'hébété,
Pour que tu puisses faire, à Jésus, quand il passe,
Un tapis triomphal avec ta charité.

Tel est l'Amour! Avant que ton cœur ne se blase,
A la gloire de Dieu rallume ton extase;
C'est la Volupté vraie aux durables appas!»

Et l'Ange, châtiant autant, ma foi! qu'il aime,
De ses poings de géant torture l'anathème;
Mais le damné répond toujours: «Je ne veux pas!»

···

The Rebel

A furious Angel swoops down like an eagle, grabs the hair of the unbeliever
in a strong fist and, shaking him, says, 'You *will* know the rule! (For I am
your good Angel, do you hear?) I insist on it!

'Understand that you must love, without shilly-shallying, the poor, the
wicked, the cripple, the feeble-minded, so that when Jesus comes you will
be able to lay down a triumphal carpet for him made of your charity.

'That is what Love is! Before your heart hardens completely, light up your
ecstasy again at the glory of God; that is real Pleasure, whose joys are
lasting.'

And the Angel, chastising, naturally, the one he loves most, with his
giant's fists tortures the reprobate, but the damned rebel always answers, 'I
won't!'

88 L'Avertisseur

Tout homme digne de ce nom
A dans le cœur un Serpent jaune,
Installé comme sur un trône,
Qui, s'il dit: «Je veux!» répond: «Non!»

Plonge tes yeux dans les yeux fixes
Des Satyresses ou des Nixes,
La Dent dit: «Pense à ton devoir!»

Fais des enfants, plante des arbres,
Polis des vers, sculpte des marbres,
La Dent dit: «Vivras-tu ce soir?»

Quoi qu'il ébauche ou qu'il espère,
L'homme ne vit pas un moment
Sans subir l'avertissement
De l'insupportable Vipère.

....

The Warning Voice

Every man worthy of the name has in his heart a yellow Serpent, set in place as if on a throne, who, if ever he says, 'I want!', replies 'No.'

Gaze into the steady eyes of Satyresses or Water-nymphs, the Tooth says, 'Think of your duty.'

Beget children, plant trees, polish verses, carve marble, the Tooth says, 'Will you still be alive this evening?'

Whatever he attempts or hopes for, man does not live for a moment without suffering the warning of the intolerable Viper.

89 Recueillement

Sois sage, ô ma Douleur, et tiens-toi plus tranquille.
Tu réclamais le Soir; il descend; le voici:
Une atmosphère obscure enveloppe la ville,
Aux uns portant la paix, aux autres le souci.

Pendant que des mortels la multitude vile,
Sous le fouet du Plaisir, ce bourreau sans merci,
Va cueillir des remords dans la fête servile,
Ma Douleur, donne-moi la main; viens par ici,

Loin d'eux. Vois se pencher les défuntes Années,
Sur les balcons du ciel, en robes surannées;
Surgir du fond des eaux le Regret souriant;

Le Soleil moribond s'endormir sous une arche,
Et, comme un long linceul traînant à l'Orient,
Entends, ma chère, entends la douce Nuit qui marche.

....

Self-Communion

Calm down, Sorrow dear, and be at peace; you said you wanted Evening;
it's coming; here it is: a shadowy atmosphere is enfolding the city, bringing
peace to some and to others cares.

While the vile throng of mortals, flying before the whip of Pleasure, that
merciless torturer, goes gathering remorse in the slavish carnival, you,
Sorrow dear, give me your hand, come over here,

Away from them. Look, see the departed Years leaning out from the
balconies of heaven, in old-fashioned dresses; see, rising from the depths of
the waters, smiling Regret;

The dying Sun going to sleep under an arch, and, like a long shroud
trailing in the East, listen, darling, listen to soft Night approaching.

90 Les Plaintes d'un Icare

Les amants des prostituées
Sont heureux, dispos et repus;
Quant à moi, mes bras sont rompus
Pour avoir étreint des nuées.

C'est grâce aux astres nonpareils,
Qui tout au fond du ciel flamboient,
Que mes yeux consumés ne voient
Que des souvenirs de soleils.

En vain j'ai voulu de l'espace
Trouver la fin et le milieu;
Sous je ne sais quel œil de feu
Je sens mon aile qui se casse;

Et brûlé par l'amour du beau,
Je n'aurai pas l'honneur sublime
De donner mon nom à l'abîme ˙
Qui me servira de tombeau.

....

The Complaints of an Icarus

The lovers of prostitutes are happy, healthy and sated; as for me, my arms
are broken from having embraced clouds.

It's thanks to the matchless stars that blaze in the furthest skies that my
burnt-out eyes now see only memories of suns.

In vain I tried to find the limits and centre of space; under some unknown
fiery eye I feel my wing breaking;

And, consumed by the love of the beautiful, I shall not have the sublime
honour of giving my name to the abyss that will be my tomb.

91   L'Examen de Minuit

La pendule, sonnant minuit,
Ironiquement nous engage
A nous rappeler quel usage
Nous fîmes du jour qui s'enfuit:
– Aujourd'hui, date fatidique,
Vendredi, treize, nous avons,
Malgré tout ce que nous savons,
Mené le train d'un hérétique.

Nous avons blasphémé Jésus,
Des Dieux le plus incontestable!
Comme un parasite à la table
De quelque monstrueux Crésus,
Nous avons, pour plaire à la brute,
Digne vassale des Démons,
Insulté ce que nous aimons
Et flatté ce qui nous rebute;

....

The Midnight Examination

The clock, striking midnight, ironically invites us to recall what use we
made of the departing day. – Today, on the fateful date of Friday the
thirteenth, we, in spite of all we know, lived like a very heretic.

We blasphemed Jesus, the most undeniable of Gods; like a parasite at the
table of some monstrous Croesus, we, to please the brute, worthy vassal of
the Demons, insulted what we love and flattered what disgusts us;

Contristé, servile bourreau,
Le faible qu'à tort on méprise;
Salué l'énorme Bêtise,
La Bêtise au front de taureau;
Baisé la stupide Matière
Avec grande dévotion,
Et de la putréfaction
Béni la blafarde lumière.

Enfin, nous avons, pour noyer
Le vertige dans le délire,
Nous, prêtre orgueilleux de la Lyre,
Dont la gloire est de déployer
L'ivresse des choses funèbres,
Bu sans soif et mangé sans faim! . . .
– Vite soufflons la lampe, afin
De nous cacher dans les ténèbres!

....

A slavish torturer, we brought sadness to the poor man who is unjustly despised; we saluted enormous Stupidity, Stupidity with its bull's forehead; we kissed dumb Matter with great devotion, and, faced with putrefaction, blessed its pale light.

Finally, to drown vertigo in delirium, we, proud priest of the Lyre, whose glory it is to unfold the rapture of death and its appurtenances, instead drank without thirst and ate without hunger! . . . Quick, blow out the lamp and let us hide our shame in the darkness!

OTHER VERSE POEMS

Je n'ai pas pour maîtresse une lionne illustre:
La gueuse, de mon âme, emprunte tout son lustre;·
Invisible aux regards de l'univers moqueur,
Sa beauté ne fleurit que dans mon triste cœur.

Pour avoir des souliers elle a vendu son âme;
Mais le bon Dieu rirait si, près de cette infâme,
Je tranchais du Tartufe et singeais la hauteur,
Moi qui vends ma pensée et qui veux être auteur.

Vice beaucoup plus grave, elle porte perruque.
Tous ses beaux cheveux noirs ont fui sa blanche nuque;
Ce qui n'empêche pas les baisers amoureux
De pleuvoir sur son front plus pelé qu'un lépreux.

....

92

My mistress is no society star: if she glitters, the tramp, it's in the light
reflected from my soul; invisible to the eyes of the mocking universe, her
beauty flowers only in my sad heart.

To buy shoes she sold her soul; but God above would laugh if, when I
am with this disgraced creature, I played the hypocrite and affected high
principles, when I sell my mind and want to be an author.

What is much worse, she wears a wig. All her beautiful black hair has fled
her white nape; but that does not stop amorous kisses from raining on her
forehead, balder than a leper.

Elle louche, et l'effet de ce regard étrange
Qu'ombragent des cils noirs plus longs que ceux d'un ange,
Est tel que tous les yeux pour qui l'on s'est damné
Ne valent pas pour moi son œil juif et cerné.

Elle n'a que vingt ans; la gorge déjà basse
Pend de chaque côté comme une calebasse,
Et pourtant, me traînant chaque nuit sur son corps,
Ainsi qu'un nouveau-né, je la tette et la mords;

Et bien qu'elle n'ait pas souvent même une obole
Pour se frotter la chair et pour s'oindre l'épaule,
Je la lèche en silence avec plus de ferveur
Que Madeleine en feu les deux pieds du Sauveur.

La pauvre créature, au plaisir essoufflée,
A de rauques hoquets la poitrine gonflée,
Et je devine au bruit de son souffle brutal
Qu'elle a souvent mordu le pain de l'hôpital.

....

She squints, and the effect of her strange look, shaded by black lashes longer than an angel's, is such that all the eyes for which men have damned themselves cannot equal, for me, her Jewish eye with its black circle.

She is only twenty; her already fallen bosom hangs down on both sides like a gourd, and still, dragging myself over her body each night, like a newborn baby I suck it and bite it;

And even though she often does not have even a copper coin to rub her flesh and to grease her shoulder, I lick her silently, with more fervour than the burning Magdalen the Saviour's two feet.

The poor creature, breathless with pleasure, has her chest swollen with hoarse hiccups, and I can tell from the sound of her rough breath that she has often bitten the bread of the poor-hospital.

Ses grands yeux inquiets, durant la nuit cruelle,
Croient voir deux autres yeux au fond de la ruelle,
Car, ayant trop ouvert son cœur à tous venants,
Elle a peur sans lumière et croit aux revenants.

Ce qui fait que de suif elle use plus de livres
Qu'un vieux savant couché jour et nuit sur ses livres,
Et redoute bien moins la faim et ses tourments
Que l'apparition de ses défunts amants.

Si vous la rencontrez, bizarrement parée,
Se faufilant, au coin d'une rue égarée,
Et la tête et l'œil bas comme un pigeon blessé,
Traînant dans les ruisseaux un talon déchaussé,

Messieurs, ne crachez pas de jurons ni d'ordure
Au visage fardé de cette pauvre impure
Que déesse Famine a, par un soir d'hiver,
Contrainte à relever ses jupons en plein air.

....

Her wide-open, anxious eyes, during the cruel night, imagine they see two other eyes in the space beside the bed, for, having opened her heart too often to all comers, she is afraid of the dark and believes in ghosts.

That's why she gets through more pounds of tallow than an old scholar bent day and night over his books, and fears hunger and its torments much less than the apparition of her dead lovers.

If you meet her, bizarrely got up, slipping by, round the corner of some forgotten street, carrying her head and eye low like a wounded pigeon and dragging a bare foot in the gutters,

Gentlemen, do not spit oaths or foul words in the painted face of this poor fallen creature whom the goddess Famine reduced, one winter evening, to raising her skirts in the open air.

Cette bohème-là, c'est mon tout, ma richesse,
Ma perle, mon bijou, ma reine, ma duchesse,
Celle qui m'a bercé sur son giron vainqueur,
Et qui dans ses deux mains a réchauffé mon cœur.

93 [Drafts for an epilogue to the edition of 1861]

[i] ÉPILOGUE

Le cœur content, je suis monté sur la montagne
D'où l'on peut contempler la ville en son ampleur,
Hôpital, lupanar, purgatoire, enfer, bagne,

Où toute énormité fleurit comme une fleur.
Tu sais bien, ô Satan, patron de ma détresse,
Que je n'allais pas là pour répandre un vain pleur;

Mais, comme un vieux paillard d'une vieille maîtresse,
Je voulais m'enivrer de l'énorme catin,
Dont le charme infernal me rajeunit sans cesse.

That gypsy that you see is my everything, my treasure, my pearl, my jewel, my queen, my duchess; it is she who rocked me on her all-conquering lap and, between her two hands, warmed my heart back to life.

[i] EPILOGUE
Content at heart, I went up into the high place from where one can look down on the whole expanse of the city, poor-hospital, brothel, purgatory, hell, prison,

Where every outrage flourishes like a flower. You know, o Satan, patron of my distress, that I did not go there to shed an idle tear,

But, like on old lecher with an old mistress, I wanted to drink deep of the immense whore, whose hellish charm never fails to restore me to youth.

Que tu dormes encor dans les draps du matin,
Lourde, obscure, enrhumée, ou que tu te pavanes
Dans les voiles du soir passementés d'or fin,

Je t'aime, ô capitale infâme! Courtisanes
Et bandits, tels souvent vous offrez des plaisirs
Que ne comprennent pas les vulgaires profanes.

[ii]

[. . .]

Anges revêtus d'or, de pourpre et d'hyacinthe,
O vous! soyez témoins que j'ai fait mon devoir
Comme un parfait chimiste et comme une âme sainte.
    Car j'ai de chaque chose extrait la quintessence,
Tu m'as donné ta boue et j'en ai fait de l'or.

....

Whether you are still asleep in the sheets of morning, heavy, dark, your breathing blocked, or parading in the veils of evening embroidered with fine gold,
    I love you, infamous capital! Courtesans and bandits, thus you also often offer pleasures that the common uninitiated cannot understand.

[ii]
Angels clad in gold, in crimson and in hyacinth, o you! Bear witness that I did my duty like a perfect chemist and a holy soul. For from each thing I extracted its quintessence, you [Paris] gave me your mud and of it I made gold.

PETITS POËMES
EN PROSE

94 L'Etranger

«Qui aimes-tu le mieux, homme énigmatique, dis? ton père, ta mère, ta sœur ou ton frère?

 — Je n'ai ni père, ni mère, ni sœur, ni frère.

 — Tes amis?

 — Vous vous servez là d'une parole dont le sens m'est resté jusqu'à ce jour inconnu.

 — Ta patrie?

 — J'ignore sous quelle latitude elle est située.

 — La beauté?

 — Je l'aimerais volontiers, déesse et immortelle.

 — L'or?

 — Je le hais comme vous haïssez Dieu.

....

The Stranger

'Whom do you love best, puzzling man, tell us: your father, your mother, your sister or your brother?'

'I have no father, no mother, no sister and no brother.'

'Your friends?'

'Now you are using a word whose meaning to this day remains unknown to me.'

'Your country?'

'I do not know in which latitude it lies.'

'Beauty?'

'I would willingly love her, were she a goddess and immortal.'

'Gold?'

'I hate it as you hate God.'

— Eh! qu'aimes-tu donc, extraordinaire étranger?

— J'aime les nuages . . . les nuages qui passent . . . là-bas . . . là-bas . . . les merveilleux nuages!»

95 Le *Confiteor* de L'Artiste

Que les fins de journées d'automne sont pénétrantes! Ah! pénétrantes jusqu'à la douleur! car il est de certaines sensations délicieuses dont le vague n'exclut pas l'intensité; et il n'est pas de pointe plus acérée que celle de l'Infini.

Grand délice que celui de noyer son regard dans l'immensité du ciel et de la mer! Solitude, silence, incomparable chasteté de l'azur! une petite voile frissonnante à l'horizon, et qui par sa petitesse et son isolement imite mon irrémédiable existence, mélodie monotone de la houle, toutes ces choses pensent par moi, ou je pense par elles (car dans la grandeur de la rêverie, le *moi* se perd vite!); elles pensent, dis-je, mais musicalement

·································

'What do you love then, extraordinary stranger?'

'I love the clouds . . . the passing clouds . . . there . . . there . . . the wonderful clouds!'

The Artist's *Confiteor*

The close of autumn days, how penetrating they are! Oh! Penetrating to the point of pain! For there are some delicious sensations whose vagueness does not preclude intensity; and there is no sharper point than that of the Infinite.

What delight it is to dissolve one's gaze in the immensity of the sky and the sea! Solitude, silence, incomparable chastity of the blue yonder! A little sail trembling on the horizon, in its tininess and its isolation an image of my irremediable existence, the monotonous melody of the waves, all these things are thinking through me, or I am thinking through them (for in the expanse of dreams the *self* is soon lost!); they think, I repeat, but musically

et pittoresquement, sans arguties, sans syllogismes, sans déductions.

Toutefois, ces pensées, qu'elles sortent de moi ou s'élancent des choses, deviennent bientôt trop intenses. L'énergie dans la volupté crée un malaise et une souffrance positive. Mes nerfs trop tendus ne donnent plus que des vibrations criardes et douloureuses.

Et maintenant la profondeur du ciel me consterne; sa limpidité m'exaspère. L'insensibilité de la mer, l'immuabilité du spectacle, me révoltent ... Ah! faut-il éternellement souffrir, ou fuir éternellement le beau? Nature, enchanteresse sans pitié, rivale toujours victorieuse, laisse-moi! Cesse de tenter mes désirs et mon orgueil! L'étude du beau est un duel où l'artiste crie de frayeur avant d'être vaincu.

....

and in a painterly fashion, without clever points, without syllogisms, without inferences.

All the same, these thoughts, whether they come from me or spring out of things, soon become too intense. Violent pleasure creates a feeling of sickness and positive suffering. My nerves, too tense, now produce only shrill and painful vibrations.

And now the depth of the sky appals me; its limpidity enrages me. The unfeeling sea, the unchanging spectacle, revolt me ... Oh! must one suffer eternally, or eternally flee the beautiful? Nature, pitiless enchantress, ever-victorious rival, leave me alone! Stop tempting my desires and my pride! The study of the beautiful is a duel in which the artist cries out in fear before being defeated.

96 La Chambre Double

Une chambre qui ressemble à une rêverie, une chambre véritablement *spirituelle*, où l'atmosphère stagnante est légèrement teintée de rose et de bleu.

L'âme y prend un bain de paresse, aromatisé par le regret et le désir. – C'est quelque chose de crépusculaire, de bleuâtre et de rosâtre; un rêve de volupté pendant une éclipse.

Les meubles ont des formes allongées, prostrées, alanguies. Les meubles ont l'air de rêver; on les dirait doués d'une vie somnambulique, comme le végétal et le minéral. Les étoffes parlent une langue muette, comme les fleurs, comme les ciels, comme les soleils couchants.

Sur les murs nulle abomination artistique. Relativement au rêve pur, à l'impression non analysée, l'art défini, l'art positif est un blasphème. Ici, tout a la suffisante clarté et la délicieuse obscurité de l'harmonie.

Une senteur infinitésimale du choix le plus exquis, à laquelle se mêle une très légère humidité, nage dans cette atmosphère,

....

The Double Room

A room which is like a dream, a truly *spiritual* room, where the enclosed atmosphere is lightly tinged with pink and with blue.

Here the soul bathes in idleness, scented with regret and desire. It has something of twilight, bluish, pinkish; a dream of pleasure during an eclipse.

The forms of the furniture are lengthened, prostrate, languid. The pieces of furniture seem to be dreaming; you would imagine that they were endowed with a kind of sleepwalking life, like plants and stones. The fabrics speak a silent language, like the flowers, like the skies, like the setting suns.

On the walls no artistic abominations. Compared to the pure dream, the unanalysed impression, definite art, positive art is a blasphemy. Here everything has the sufficient clarity and the delicious obscurity of harmony.

A barely perceptible scent of the most exquisite choosing, with which

où l'esprit sommeillant est bercé par des sensations de serre chaude.

La mousseline pleut abondamment devant les fenêtres et devant le lit; elle s'épanche en cascades neigeuses. Sur ce lit est couchée l'Idole, la souveraine des rêves. Mais comment est-elle ici? Qui l'a amenée? quel pouvoir magique l'a installée sur ce trône de rêverie et de volupté? Qu'importe? la voilà! je la reconnais.

Voilà bien ces yeux dont la flamme traverse le crépuscule; ces subtiles et terribles *mirettes*, que je reconnais à leur effrayante malice! Elles attirent, elles subjuguent, elles dévorent le regard de l'imprudent qui les contemple. Je les ai souvent étudiées, ces étoiles noires qui commandent la curiosité et l'admiration.

A quel démon bienveillant dois-je d'être ainsi entouré de mystère, de silence, de paix et de parfums? O béatitude! ce que nous nommons généralement la vie, même dans son expansion la plus heureuse, n'a rien de commun avec cette vie suprême dont j'ai maintenant connaissance et que je savoure minute par minute, seconde par seconde!

....

is mingled a very slight moistness, floats in this atmosphere, in which the drowsy spirit is cradled as if in sensations of a hothouse.

Muslin falls in abundance before the windows and before the bed; it flows in snowy cascades. On this bed lies the Idol, the queen of dreams. But how has she come here? Who has brought her? What magic power has set her on this throne of dreams and pleasure? What does it matter? She is here! I recognize her.

Yes, those are her eyes whose flame burns through the twilight; those subtle and terrible *peepers*, which I know by their frightening mischievousness! They attract, they conquer, they devour the look of the imprudent man who gazes on them. I have often studied them, those black stars commanding curiosity and admiration.

What benevolent spirit has thus surrounded me with mystery, silence, peace and perfumes? O blessedness! What we usually call life, even in its widest span of happiness, has nothing in common with this supreme life which I have now come to know and which I am savouring minute by minute, second by second!

Non! il n'est plus de minutes, il n'est plus de secondes! Le temps a disparu; c'est l'Éternité qui règne, une éternité de délices!

Mais un coup terrible, lourd, a retenti à la porte, et, comme dans les rêves infernaux, il m'a semblé que je recevais un coup de pioche dans l'estomac.

Et puis un Spectre est entré. C'est un huissier qui vient me torturer au nom de la loi; une infâme concubine qui vient crier misère et ajouter les trivialités de sa vie aux douleurs de la mienne; ou bien le saute-ruisseau d'un directeur de journal qui réclame la suite du manuscrit.

La chambre paradisiaque, l'idole, la souveraine des rêves, la *Sylphide*, comme disait le grand René, toute cette magie a disparu au coup brutal frappé par le Spectre.

Horreur! je me souviens! je me souviens! Oui! ce taudis, ce séjour de l'éternel ennui, est bien le mien. Voici les meubles sots, poudreux, écornés; la cheminée sans flamme et sans braise, souillée de crachats; les tristes fenêtres où la pluie a tracé des sillons dans la poussière; les manuscrits, raturés ou incomplets; l'almanach où le crayon a marqué les dates sinistres!

....

No! there are no more minutes, no more seconds! Time has disappeared; Eternity reigns, an eternity of delight!

But a terrible, loud knock has sounded at the door and, as in hellish dreams, I felt that a pick was being driven into my stomach.

And then a Spectre entered. It is a bailiff who has come to torture me in the name of the law; a wretched concubine come to cry poverty and add the trivial concerns of her life to the sufferings of mine; or an editor's errand-boy come to demand the rest of the manuscript.

The heavenly room, the idol, the queen of dreams, the *Sylph* as great René called her, all the magic disappeared at the Spectre's brutal knock.

Horror! I remember! I remember! Yes! this slum room, this dwelling of eternal ennui, is mine. Here is the stupid furniture, dusty, battered; the fireplace without flame and without embers, soiled with spittle; the dull windows where the rain has traced furrows in the dust; the manuscripts, covered with crossings-out or unfinished; the calendar with pencil markings on the most dreaded dates!

Et ce parfum d'un autre monde, dont je m'enivrais avec une sensibilité perfectionnée, hélas! il est remplacé par une fétide odeur de tabac mêlée à je ne sais quelle nauséabonde moisissure. On respire ici maintenant le ranci de la désolation.

Dans ce monde étroit, mais si plein de dégoût, un seul objet connu me sourit: la fiole de laudanum; une vieille et terrible amie; comme toutes les amies, hélas! féconde en caresses et en traîtrises.

Oh! oui! le Temps a reparu; le Temps règne en souverain maintenant; et avec le hideux vieillard est revenu tout son démoniaque cortège de Souvenirs, de Regrets, de Spasmes, de Peurs, d'Angoisses, de Cauchemars, de Colères et de Névroses.

Je vous assure que les secondes maintenant sont fortement et solennellement accentuées, et chacune, en jaillissant de la pendule, dit: – «Je suis la Vie, l'insupportable, l'implacable Vie!»

Il n'y a qu'une Seconde dans la vie humaine qui ait mission d'annoncer une bonne nouvelle, la *bonne nouvelle* qui cause à chacun une inexplicable peur.

....

And that perfume from another world, intoxicating to my sharpened senses, alas, is replaced by a fetid stink of tobacco mixed with a nameless, nauseating smell of mould. One breathes in, here, now, the sourness of desolation.

In this world, narrow but so full of disgust, only one known object smiles at me: the laudanum flask; an old and terrible friend; and like all women friends, alas, rich in caresses and in treacheries.

Yes indeed! Time has returned; Time is king now; and with the hideous old man there has returned his whole devilish cortège of Memories, Regrets, Shudders, Fears, Tremblings, Nightmares, Rages and Neuroses.

I can assure you that the seconds are heavily and solemnly marked now, and each one, as it springs from the clock, says: 'I am Life, intolerable, implacable Life!'

There is only one Second in all human life whose mission it is to announce good news, that very *good news* which causes everyone such inexplicable fear.

Oui! le Temps règne; il a repris sa brutale dictature. Et il me pousse, comme si j'étais un bœuf, avec son double aiguillon. – «Et hue donc! bourrique! Sue donc, esclave! Vis donc, damné!»

97 Le Chien et le Flacon

«– Mon beau chien, mon bon chien, mon cher toutou, approchez et venez respirer un excellent parfum acheté chez le meilleur parfumeur de la ville.»

Et le chien, en frétillant de la queue, ce qui est, je crois, chez ces pauvres êtres, le signe correspondant du rire et du sourire, s'approche et pose curieusement son nez humide sur le flacon débouché; puis, reculant soudainement avec effroi, il aboie contre moi, en manière de reproche.

«– Ah! misérable chien, si je vous avais offert un paquet d'excréments, vous l'auriez flairé avec délices et peut-être dévoré. Ainsi, vous-même, indigne compagnon de ma triste vie, vous ressemblez au public, à qui il ne faut jamais présenter

....

Yes! Time reigns; he has resumed his brutal dictatorship. And he pushes me, as if I were an ox, with his double goad. 'Gee up, then, donkey! Sweat, then, slave! Live, then, damned victim!'

The Dog and the Scent-bottle

'Nice dog, good dog, dear doggie, come and smell some excellent scent from the best shop in town.'

And the dog, wagging its tail, which is, I think, in these poor creatures, the sign corresponding to laughter or smiling, comes up and applies its wet nose, curiously, to the open bottle; then, starting back in fear, barks at me reproachfully.

'Wretched dog! If I had offered you a pile of excrement, you would have sniffed it delightedly and perhaps eaten it. Thus even you, unworthy companion of my unhappy life, are like the public, to whom one

des parfums délicats qui l'exaspèrent, mais des ordures soigneuse-
ment choisies.»

98 A Une Heure du Matin

Enfin! seul! On n'entend plus que le roulement de quelques
fiacres attardés et éreintés. Pendant quelques heures, nous
posséderons le silence, sinon le repos. Enfin! la tyrannie de la
face humaine a disparu, et je ne souffrirai plus que par moi-
même.

Enfin! il m'est donc permis de me délasser dans un bain de
ténèbres! D'abord, un double tour à la serrure. Il me semble
que ce tour de clef augmentera ma solitude et fortifiera les
barricades qui me séparent actuellement du monde.

Horrible vie! Horrible ville! Récapitulons la journée: avoir
vu plusieurs hommes de lettres, dont l'un m'a demandé si l'on
pouvait aller en Russie par voie de terre (il prenait sans doute
la Russie pour une île); avoir disputé généreusement contre
le directeur d'une revue, qui à chaque objection répondait:

....

must never offer delicate scents which enrage it, but carefully selected
ordure.'

At One O'clock in the Morning

At last! alone! There is nothing to be heard but the wheels of a few late,
rickety passing cabs. For a few hours now we shall be in possession of
silence, if not of rest. At last the tyranny of the human face has receded, and
I shall suffer only from my own presence.

At last! Now I can relax in a bath of darkness! First, a double turn of the
key. I feel as if this double locking will increase my solitude and strengthen
the barricades that separate me at this moment from the world.

Hideous life! Hideous city! Let us tell over the day's events: saw several
men of letters, one of whom asked me if it is possible to travel to Russia
overland (no doubt he believes Russia is an island); argued nobly against the

«— C'est ici le parti des honnêtes gens», ce qui implique que tous les autres journaux sont rédigés par des coquins; avoir salué une vingtaine de personnes, dont quinze me sont inconnues; avoir distribué des poignées de main dans la même proportion, et cela sans avoir pris la précaution d'acheter des gants; être monté pour tuer le temps, pendant une averse, chez une sauteuse qui m'a prié de lui dessiner un costume de *Vénustre;* avoir fait ma cour à un directeur de théâtre, qui m'a dit en me congédiant: «— Vous feriez peut-être bien de vous adresser à Z . . .; c'est le plus lourd, le plus sot et le plus célèbre de tous mes auteurs, avec lui vous pourriez peut-être aboutir à quelque chose. Voyez-le, et puis nous verrons»; m'être vanté (pourquoi?) de plusieurs vilaines actions que je n'ai jamais commises, et avoir lâchement nié quelques autres méfaits que j'ai accomplis avec joie, délit de fanfaronnade, crime de respect humain; avoir refusé à un ami un service facile, et donné une recommandation écrite à un parfait drôle; ouf! est-ce bien fini?

Mécontent de tous et mécontent de moi, je voudrais bien me racheter et m'enorgueillir un peu dans le silence et la

....

editor of a magazine, who to each of my objections replied: 'We're not decent people here,' thus implying that all the other papers are written by rogues; greeted twenty-odd people, fifteen of whom are unknown to me; shook hands on the same scale, and that without having taken the precaution of buying gloves; went up to a dancer's flat to kill time, during a shower of rain: she asked me to design her a costume as *Vénustre*; made up to a theatre manager, who said as he showed me out, 'You should perhaps try approaching Z—; he's the least inspired, the stupidest and the most famous of my authors; if you worked with him you might perhaps get somewhere. See him, and then we'll talk'; boasted (why?) of several ugly actions I have never committed, and cravenly denied certain other misdeeds that I carried out with joy: a sin of vainglory and a crime of human respect; refused a friend a simple favour and wrote a letter of recommendation for a downright crook; help! is that all?

Dissatisfied with everyone and dissatisfied with myself, I long to redeem myself and regain some pride in the silence and solitude of the night. Souls

solitude de la nuit. Ames de ceux que j'ai aimés, âmes de ceux que j'ai chantés, fortifiez-moi, soutenez-moi, éloignez de moi le mensonge et les vapeurs corruptrices du monde, et vous, Seigneur mon Dieu! accordez-moi la grâce de produire quelques beaux vers qui me prouvent à moi-même que je ne suis pas le dernier des hommes, que je ne suis pas inférieur à ceux que je méprise!

99 Les Foules

Il n'est pas donné à chacun de prendre un bain de multitude: jouir de la foule est un art; et celui-là seul peut faire, aux dépens du genre humain, une ribote de vitalité, à qui une fée a insufflé dans son berceau le goût du travestissement et du masque, la haine du domicile et la passion du voyage.

Multitude, solitude: termes égaux et convertibles pour le poète actif et fécond. Qui ne sait pas peupler sa solitude, ne sait pas non plus être seul dans une foule affairée.

....

of those I have loved, souls of those of whom I have sung, strengthen me, bear me up, protect me from lies and from the corrupting vapours of this world, and you, o Lord, my God! give me the grace to produce some fine lines of verse that may prove to myself that I am not the lowest of the low, not a lesser thing than those I despise.

Crowds

Not everyone has the gift of bathing in the multitude; taking pleasure in the crowd is an art; and the only man who can use the human race to binge on life-energy is the one into whom a fairy breathed, when he was in his cradle, a taste for disguises and masks, hatred of home and a passion for travel.

Multitude, solitude: equal and interchangeable terms for the active, fertile poet. The man who cannot people his solitude will not be able, either, to be alone in a busy crowd.

Le poète jouit de cet incomparable privilège, qu'il peut à sa guise être lui-même et autrui. Comme ces âmes errantes qui cherchent un corps, il entre, quand il veut, dans le personnage de chacun. Pour lui seul, tout est vacant; et si de certaines places paraissent lui êtres fermées, c'est qu'à ses yeux elles ne valent pas la peine d'être visitées.

Le promeneur solitaire et pensif tire une singulière ivresse de cette universelle communion. Celui-là qui épouse facilement la foule connaît des jouissances fiévreuses, dont seront éternellement privé l'égoïste, fermé comme un coffre, et le paresseux, interné comme un mollusque. Il adopte comme siennes toutes les professions, toutes les joies et toutes les misères que la circonstance lui présente.

Ce que les hommes nomment amour est bien petit, bien restreint et bien faible, comparé à cette ineffable orgie, à cette sainte prostitution de l'âme qui se donne tout entière, poésie et charité, à l'imprévu qui se montre, à l'inconnu qui passe.

Il est bon d'apprendre quelquefois aux heureux de ce monde, ne fût-ce que pour humilier un instant leur sot

---

The poet enjoys the incomparable privilege of being able at will to be himself and someone else. Like wandering souls seeking a body, he enters, when he pleases, the personality of anyone and everyone. For him alone, everything lies open; and if some places seem to be closed to him, that is because, in his eyes, they are not worth visiting.

The solitary, thoughtful walker draws a singular excitement from this universal communion. He who can easily match himself to the crowd knows feverish pleasures of which the egoist, shut up like a trunk, and the lazy man, inward-turning as a mollusc, will for ever be deprived. He takes for his own all the professions, all the joys and all the wretchedness that circumstances present to him.

What men call love is a very small thing, very restricted and very feeble, compared to this inexpressible orgy, this holy prostitution of the soul which gives itself up entirely, poetry and charity, to the unexpected as it appears, the stranger passing by.

It is good now and then to show the fortunate ones in this world (if only to cast down for a moment their stupid pride) that there are happinesses

orgueil, qu'il est des bonheurs supérieurs au leur, plus vastes et plus raffinés. Les fondateurs de colonies, les pasteurs de peuples, les prêtres missionnaires exilés au bout du monde, connaissent sans doute quelque chose de ces mystérieuses ivresses; et, au sein de la vaste famille que leur génie s'est faite, ils doivent rire quelquefois de ceux qui les plaignent pour leur fortune si agitée et pour leur vie si chaste.

100 Un Cheval de Race

Elle est bien laide. Elle est délicieuse pourtant!

Le Temps et l'Amour l'ont marquée de leurs griffes et lui ont cruellement enseigné ce que chaque minute et chaque baiser emportent de jeunesse et de fraîcheur.

Elle est vraiment laide; elle est fourmi, araignée, si vous voulez, squelette même; mais aussi elle est breuvage, magistère, sorcellerie! en somme, elle est exquise.

Le Temps n'a pu rompre l'harmonie pétillante de sa démarche ni l'élégance indestructible de son armature. L'Amour

....

superior to theirs, vaster and subtler. The founders of colonies, shepherds of peoples, missionary priests exiled at the ends of the earth, no doubt know something of these mysterious intoxications; and, in the bosom of the vast family which their genius has made for itself, they must sometimes laugh at those who pity them for their turbulent fate and their life of such chastity.

A Thoroughbred

She really is ugly. She's delicious, though!

Time and Love have marked her with their claws and have cruelly taught her what every minute and every kiss cost in youth and freshness.

She is really ugly; she is an ant, a spider, if you like, a skeleton even; but then she is also a love potion, a word of mastery, a spell! In a word, she is exquisite.

Time has not broken the sparkling harmony of her movements nor the

n'a pas altéré la suavité de son haleine d'enfant; et le Temps n'a rien arraché de son abondante crinière d'où s'exhale en fauves parfums toute la vitalité endiablée du Midi français: Nîmes, Aix, Arles, Avignon, Narbonne, Toulouse, villes bénies du soleil, amoureuses et charmantes!

Le Temps et l'Amour l'ont vainement mordue à belles dents; ils n'ont rien diminué du charme vague, mais éternel, de sa poitrine garçonnière.

Usée peut-être, mais non fatiguée, et toujours héroïque, elle fait penser à ces chevaux de grande race que l'œil du véritable amateur reconnaît, même attelés à un carrosse de louage ou à un lourd chariot.

Et puis elle est si douce et si fervente! Elle aime comme on aime en automne; on dirait que les approches de l'hiver allument dans son cœur un feu nouveau, et la servilité de sa tendresse n'a jamais rien de fatigant.

---

indestructible elegance of her bone structure. Love has not corrupted the sweetness of her child's breath; and Time has not thinned in the slightest her abundant mane of hair, from which exudes in animal scents all the devilish vitality of the French south: Nîmes, Aix, Arles, Avignon, Narbonne, Toulouse, cities blessed by the sun, amorous and delightful!

Time and Love have sunk their teeth in her in vain; they have done nothing to lessen the vague, but eternal, charm of her boyish bosom.

Worn perhaps, but not tired, and still heroic, she makes one think of those thoroughbred horses which the connoisseur's eye can spot, even when they are harnessed to a hackney-carriage or a heavy cart.

And then she is so gentle and so passionate. She loves as one loves in autumn; you would say that the approach of winter is lighting a new fire in her heart, and the servility of her tenderness is never in the least fatiguing.

101 Any Where out of the World

N'IMPORTE OÙ HORS DU MONDE

Cette vie est un hôpital où chaque malade est possédé du désir de changer de lit. Celui-ci voudrait souffrir en face du poêle, et celui-là croit qu'il guérirait à côté de la fenêtre.

Il me semble que je serais toujours bien là où je ne suis pas, et cette question de déménagement en est une que je discute sans cesse avec mon âme.

«Dis-moi, mon âme, pauvre âme refroidie, que penserais-tu d'habiter Lisbonne? Il doit y faire chaud, et tu t'y ragaillardirais comme un lézard. Cette ville est au bord de l'eau; on dit qu'elle est bâtie en marbre, et que le peuple y a une telle haine du végétal, qu'il arrache tous les arbres. Voilà un paysage selon ton goût; un paysage fait avec la lumière et le minéral, et le liquide pour les réfléchir!»

Mon âme ne répond pas.

«Puisque tu aimes tant le repos, avec le spectacle du

....

Anywhere out of the World

This life is a poor-hospital where every patient is obsessed with the desire to change beds. One wants to suffer facing the stove, the other believes that he would get better next to the window.

I always feel that I would be better off somewhere I am not, and this question of moving is one that I am constantly discussing with my soul.

'Tell me, soul, poor chilly soul, what would you think of living in Lisbon? It must be warm there, and you would come back to life, like a lizard. The city is next to the water; they say it is built of marble, and that the people so hate anything green that they pull up all the trees. That's a landscape after your tastes; a landscape made of light and stones, with liquid to reflect them!'

My soul doesn't reply.

'Since you so love to rest and watch movement, would you like to come

mouvement, veux-tu venir habiter la Hollande, cette terre
béatifiante? Peut-être te divertiras-tu dans cette contrée dont
tu as souvent admiré l'image dans les musées. Que penserais-
tu de Rotterdam, toi qui aimes les forêts de mâts, et les
navires amarrés au pied des maisons?»

Mon âme reste muette.

«Batavia te sourirait peut-être davantage? Nous y trouveri-
ons d'ailleurs l'esprit de l'Europe marié à la beauté tropicale.»

Pas un mot. – Mon âme serait-elle morte?

«En es-tu donc venue à ce point d'engourdissement que tu
ne te plaises que dans ton mal? S'il en est ainsi, fuyons vers les
pays qui sont les analogies de la Mort.

– Je tiens notre affaire, pauvre âme! Nous ferons nos malles
pour Tornéo. Allons plus loin encore, à l'extrême bout de la
Baltique; encore plus loin de la vie, si c'est possible; installons-
nous au pôle. Là le soleil ne frise qu'obliquement la terre, et
les lentes alternatives de la lumière et de la nuit suppriment la
variété et augmentent la monotonie, cette moitié du néant.
Là, nous pourrons prendre de longs bains de ténèbres, cepend-
ant que, pour nous divertir, les aurores boréales nous enverront

....

and live in Holland, that blessed-making country? Perhaps you will find
pleasure in that land whose picture you have so often admired in museums.
What would you think of Rotterdam, you who love forests of masts, and
ships moored under the houses?'

My soul remains dumb.

'Perhaps you'd prefer Batavia? There we'd find the spirit of Europe
wedded to tropical beauty.'

Not a word. Could my soul be dead?

'Are you so benumbed that you can only take pleasure in your sickness? If
that is so, let us flee to those countries that are analogies of death.

'I know the place for us, my poor soul! We shall pack our bags for
Torneo. Let us go further still, to the far end of the Baltic; further yet from
life, if we can; let us settle at the pole. There the sun only brushes the earth
obliquely, and the slow alternation of light and darkness eliminates variety
and increases monotony, that halfway-house to nothingness. There we can
take long shadow-baths, while, for our diversion, the Northern Lights will,

de temps en temps leurs gerbes roses, comme des reflets d'un feu d'artifice de l'Enfer!»

Enfin, mon âme fait explosion, et sagement elle me crie: «N'importe où! n'importe où! pourvu que ce soit hors de ce monde!»

102 Les Bons Chiens

A M. Joseph Stevens

Je n'ai jamais rougi, même devant les jeunes écrivains de mon siècle, de mon admiration pour Buffon; mais aujourd'hui ce n'est pas l'âme de ce peintre de la nature pompeuse que j'appellerai à mon aide. Non.

Bien plus volontiers je m'adresserais à Sterne, et je lui dirais: «Descends du ciel, ou monte vers moi des champs Elyséens, pour m'inspirer en faveur des bons chiens, des pauvres chiens, un chant digne de toi, sentimental farceur, farceur incomparable! Reviens à califourchon sur ce fameux âne qui t'accompagne toujours dans la mémoire de la postérité;

....

from time to time, send us their sheaves of rosy light, like reflections of a firework display in hell!'

Finally, my soul explodes into life, and wisely cries out to me, 'Anywhere! anywhere! provided it is out of this world.'

Good Dogs

I have never blushed, even before the young writers of my century, to own my admiration for Buffon; but today it is not the soul of that painter of nature in formal dress that I shall call to my aid. No.

I would much rather turn to Sterne, and say to him, 'Come down from heaven, or rise towards me from the Elysian Fields, and inspire me to praise good dogs, poor dogs, in terms worthy of you, sentimental joker, joker beyond compare! Return, astride the famous donkey which always accompanies you in the memory of posterity, and above all, let the donkey not

et surtout que cet âne n'oublie pas de porter, délicatement suspendu entre ses lèvres, son immortel macaron!»

Arrière la muse académique! Je n'ai que faire de cette vieille bégueule. J'invoque la muse familière, la citadine, la vivante, pour qu'elle m'aide à chanter les bons chiens, les pauvres chiens, les chiens crottés, ceux-là que chacun écarte, comme pestiférés et pouilleux, excepté le pauvre dont ils sont les associés, et le poète qui les regarde d'un œil fraternel.

Fi du chien bellâtre, de ce fat quadrupède, danois, king-charles, carlin ou gredin, si enchanté de lui-même qu'il s'élance indiscrètement dans les jambes ou sur les genoux du visiteur, comme s'il était sûr de plaire, turbulent comme un enfant, sot comme une lorette, quelquefois hargneux et insolent comme un domestique! Fi surtout de ces serpents à quatre pattes, frissonnants et désœuvrés, qu'on nomme levrettes, et qui ne logent même pas dans leur museau pointu assez de flair pour suivre la piste d'un ami, ni dans leur tête aplatie assez d'intelligence pour jouer au domino!

A la niche, tous ces fatigants parasites!

....

forget to bring, delicately suspended between his lips, his immortal macaroon!'

Away with the academic muse! I have no need of her, the old prude. I call upon the familiar muse, the living, city muse, to help me sing the praises of good dogs, poor dogs, dirty dogs, the dogs everyone chases away as disease-ridden and lousy, except the poor man whose associates they are, and the poet, who looks on them with a brotherly eye.

Who cares for the handsome dog, that vain, foolish quadruped, Great Dane, King Charles spaniel, pug or rascal, so pleased with himself that he charges thoughtlessly into the legs or on to the knees of the visitor, as if he were sure of a welcome, unruly as a child, stupid as a kept woman, sometimes aggressive and insolent as a manservant! Above all, away with those serpents on four legs, shivering in their idleness, called miniature greyhounds, whose pointed muzzles do not have even the sense of smell to follow the track of a friend, nor their flattened heads enough intelligence to play dominoes!

Back to the kennel with all those tiresome parasites!

Qu'ils retournent à leur niche soyeuse et capitonnée! Je chante le chien crotté, le chien pauvre, le chien sans domicile, le chien flâneur, le chien saltimbanque, le chien dont l'instinct, comme celui du pauvre, du bohémien et de l'histrion, est merveilleusement aiguillonné par la nécessité, cette si bonne mère, cette vraie patronne des intelligences!

Je chante les chiens calamiteux, soit ceux qui errent, solitaires, dans les ravines sinueuses des immenses villes, soit ceux qui ont dit à l'homme abandonné, avec des yeux clignotants et spirituels: «Prends-moi avec toi, et de nos deux misères nous ferons peut-être une espèce de bonheur!»

«*Où vont les chiens?*» disait autrefois Nestor Roqueplan dans un immortel feuilleton qu'il a sans doute oublié, et dont moi seul, et Sainte-Beuve peut-être, nous nous souvenons encore aujourd'hui.

Où vont les chiens, dites-vous, hommes peu attentifs? Ils vont à leurs affaires.

Rendez-vous d'affaires, rendez-vous d'amour. A travers la brume, à travers la neige, à travers la crotte, sous la canicule

....

Let them go back to their silk-padded kennels! I sing the mud-stained dog, the poor dog, the homeless dog, the idling dog, the street acrobat's dog, the dog whose instinct, like that of the poor man, the gypsy and the actor, is marvellously sharpened by necessity, that good mother, that real patroness of human wit.

I sing of broken-down dogs, either those who wander alone in the twisting ravines of huge cities, or those who have said to rejected man, blinking their intelligent eyes, 'Let me be with you, and perhaps from our two wretchednesses we can make a kind of happiness!'

'*Where do dogs go?*', Nestor Roqueplan once asked in an immortal column which he has probably now forgotten, and which only I, and perhaps Sainte-Beuve, remember today.

Where are the dogs going, you ask, unobservant men? They are going about their business.

Business meetings, dates. Through the mist, through the snow, through the mud, under the biting heat of midsummer, under the pouring rain, they

mordante, sous la pluie ruisselante, ils vont, ils viennent, ils trottent, ils passent sous les voitures, excités par les puces, la passion, le besoin ou le devoir. Comme nous, ils se sont levés de bon matin, et ils cherchent leur vie ou courent à leurs plaisirs.

Il y en a qui couchent dans une ruine de la banlieue et qui viennent, chaque jour, à heure fixe, réclamer la sportule à la porte d'une cuisine du Palais-Royal; d'autres qui accourent, par troupes, de plus de cinq lieues, pour partager le repas que leur a préparé la charité de certaines pucelles sexagénaires, dont le cœur inoccupé s'est donné aux bêtes, parce que les hommes imbéciles n'en veulent plus.

D'autres qui, comme des nègres marrons, affolés d'amour, quittent, à de certains jours, leur département pour venir à la ville, gambader pendant une heure autour d'une belle chienne, un peu négligée dans sa toilette, mais fière et reconnaissante.

Et ils sont tous très exacts, sans carnets, sans notes et sans portefeuilles.

Connaissez-vous la paresseuse Belgique, et avez-vous admiré comme moi tous ces chiens vigoureux attelés à la charrette du

....

come, they go, they trot along, they pass under the carriages, spurred on by fleas, passion, need or duty. Like us, they got up early and they are seeking their livelihood or running after their pleasures.

Some of them sleep in a ruined building in the outskirts and come every day at a set hour to claim their dole at the door of a kitchen in the Palais-Royal; others come in bands from more than thirty miles away to share the meal prepared for them by the charity of certain sexagenarian virgins, whose unclaimed heart has given itself to animals, since men in their stupidity no longer want it.

Others, like runaway slaves, maddened by love, leave, on certain days, their *département* to come to the town and gambol for an hour around a beautiful bitch, not very well presented but proud and grateful for their attention.

And they're all perfectly punctual, without diaries, notebooks or wallets.

Do you know Belgium, that lazy country, and have you, like me,

boucher, de la laitière ou du boulanger, et qui témoignent, par leurs aboiements triomphants, du plaisir orgueilleux qu'ils éprouvent à rivaliser avec les chevaux?

En voici deux qui appartiennent à un ordre encore plus civilisé! Permettez-moi de vous introduire dans la chambre du saltimbanque absent. Un lit, en bois peint, sans rideaux, des couvertures traînantes et souillées de punaises, deux chaises de paille, un poêle de fonte, un ou deux instruments de musique détraqués. Oh! le triste mobilier! Mais regardez, je vous prie, ces deux personnages intelligents, habillés de vêtements à la fois éraillés et somptueux, coiffés comme des troubadours ou des militaires, qui surveillent, avec une attention de sorciers, *l'œuvre sans nom* qui mitonne sur le poêle allumé, et au centre de laquelle une longue cuiller se dresse, plantée comme un de ces mâts aériens qui annoncent que la maçonnerie est achevée.

N'est-il pas juste que de si zélés comédiens ne se mettent pas en route sans avoir lesté leur estomac d'une soupe puissante et solide? Et ne pardonnerez-vous pas un peu de sensualité à ces pauvres diables qui ont à affronter tout le jour

....

admired all those strong, lively dogs yoked to the butcher's, milk-woman's or baker's carts, showing by their exultant barking the pleasure and pride they take in rivalling the horses?

Here are two belonging to an even more civilized order! Allow me to take you into the room of the absent street acrobat. A bed of painted wood, without curtains, bedbug-stained blankets trailing on the floor, two rush-seated chairs, a cast-iron stove, one or two broken musical instruments. What sad furnishings! But look, if you will, at these two intelligent figures, dressed in worn but sumptuous garments, with troubadours' or soldiers' caps, watching with a wizard's attentiveness the *nameless work* simmering on the lighted stove, and in the middle of which a long spoon stands upright, like one of those mid-air masts that mark the completion of a building.

Isn't it right that such keen actors should not set out without having put something solid in their stomachs: a powerful, thick soup? And won't you forgive a little sensual yearning in these poor devils who have to spend all day

l'indifférence du public et les injustices d'un directeur qui se fait la grosse part et mange à lui seul plus de soupe que quatre comédiens?

Que de fois j'ai contemplé, souriant et attendri, tous ces philosophes à quatre pattes, esclaves complaisants, soumis ou dévoués, que le dictionnaire républicain pourrait aussi bien qualifier d'*officieux*, si la république, trop occupée du *bonheur* des hommes, avait le temps de ménager l'*honneur* des chiens!

Et que de fois j'ai pensé qu'il y avait peut-être quelque part (qui sait, après tout?), pour récompenser tant de courage, tant de patience et de labeur, un paradis spécial pour les bons chiens, les pauvres chiens, les chiens crottés et désolés. Swedenborg affirme bien qu'il y en a un pour les Turcs et un pour les Hollandais!

Les bergers de Virgile et de Théocrite attendaient, pour prix de leurs chants alternés, un bon fromage, une flûte du meilleur faiseur, ou une chèvre aux mamelles gonflées. Le poète qui a chanté les pauvres chiens a reçu pour récompense un beau gilet, d'une couleur, à la fois riche et fanée, qui fait

....

facing the indifference of the public and the unjust treatment of a director who takes the lion's share for himself and eats up more soup than four actors put together?

How often I have watched, smiling and touched, all those four-legged philosophers, indulgent slaves, submissive or devoted, whom the republican dictionary could also call *dutiful*, if only the republic, too busy with the *happiness* of the citizens, could find time to show respect for the *honour* of dogs!

And how often I have thought that perhaps somewhere (who knows, after all) there was a reward for such courage, such patience and hard work, a special paradise for the good dogs, the poor dogs, the dirty, muddy, sad and sorry dogs. After all, Swedenborg says there is one for Turks and one for Dutchmen!

The shepherds in Virgil and Theocritus hoped their amoebean verses would win them a good cheese, a flute from the best maker or a she-goat with swollen udders. The poet who sang the praises of the good dogs received as his reward a beautiful waistcoat of a colour both rich and faded

penser aux soleils d'automne, à la beauté des femmes mûres et aux étés de la Saint-Martin.

Aucun de ceux qui étaient présents dans la taverne de la rue Villa-Hermosa n'oubliera avec quelle pétulance le peintre s'est dépouillé de son gilet en faveur du poète, tant il a bien compris qu'il était bon et honnête de chanter les pauvres chiens.

Tel un magnifique tyran italien, du bon temps, offrait au divin Arétin soit une dague enrichie de pierreries, soit un manteau de cour, en échange d'un précieux sonnet ou d'un curieux poème satirique.

Et toutes les fois que le poète endosse le gilet du peintre, il est contraint de penser aux bons chiens, aux chiens philosophes, aux étés de la Saint-Martin et à la beauté des femmes très mûres.

....

which recalls autumn suns, the beauty of mature women and Indian summers.

No one who was present in the tavern in the rue Villa-Hermosa will forget the impetuous dash with which the painter stripped off his waistcoat to give it to the poet, so well did he understand that it was a good and honourable thing to sing the praises of poor dogs.

Even so a magnificent Italian tyrant, in the good old days, would give to the divine Aretino perhaps a dagger set with jewels, or a court mantle, in exchange for a precious sonnet or a curious satirical poem.

And every time the poet puts on the painter's waistcoat, he cannot but think of the good dogs, the dog philosophers, of Indian summers and of the beauty of women well past their prime.

GLOSSARY

ANDROMAQUE. Andromache, wife of Hector in the *Iliad*, also known to French readers as the heroine of one of Racine's greatest plays. After the sack of Troy she was taken prisoner by Pyrrhus and later, in some versions of the story, was married off to Helenus. In 53, Baudelaire is following Virgil, *Aeneid* III, 294–318.

ANTIOPE. Antiope, in Greek legend, was an Amazon defeated by Hercules. But the definite article in 78 (*l'*Antiope) suggests rather a painting of Antiope, probably by Correggio, Watteau or Ingres.

ANTOINE. In Christian legend this saint, a desert hermit, was tempted by various alluring visions. 'The Temptations of St Anthony' was a favoured subject in sixteenth-century painting, and surfaces again in French writing of the nineteenth century. Flaubert wrote two prose narratives called *La Tentation de Saint Antoine*.

ARETINO. Pietro Aretino (1492–1556), Italian poet and prose writer, satirist and pornographer.

BOUCHER. François Boucher (1703–70), painter of elegant, often erotic subjects.

BUFFON. Georges-Louis Leclerc de Buffon (1707–88), naturalist, author of the monumental *Histoire naturelle*. His measured, elaborate and polished style gave rise to the legend that he never wrote without putting on full, formal dress, including lace jabot and wrist frills.

CAPOUE. Capua, near Naples. Hannibal delayed there instead of marching on Rome; hence, proverbially, a city of comfort and pleasure.

CARROUSEL. The Place du Carrousel, between the Louvre and the Tuileries palace (now the Tuileries garden) was opened up in 1852 by demolishing several streets of old buildings.

CÉLIMÈNE. Fashionable, flirtatious heroine of Molière's play *Le Misanthrope*.

CIRCÉ. Circe, an enchantress in the *Odyssey* who turned men into animals.

CONFITEOR. 'I confess'. Opening word of the general confession of sins in the Mass, it can also be a profession of faith, as in the Creed (*confiteor unum baptisma in remissionem peccatorum*, 'I confess one baptism for the remission of sins').

CRÉSUS. Croesus, King of Lydia (sixth century BC). Proverbial for his riches. Hence *un Crésus*, a very rich man.

CUL-DE-LAMPE. Engraved illustration, usually coming at the end of a chapter.

CYBÈLE. Cybele, often called 'the Mother of the Gods' or 'the Great Mother', was the personification of nature's powers of growth.

CYTHÈRE. Cythera, an island near Crete, site of a temple to Venus. Proverbially the abode of love. 'The Embarkation for Cythera', a favoured subject for painters, notably Watteau (1684–1721), stood metaphorically for the beginning of a love affair.

DAVID. When David, King of Israel, was 'old and stricken in years', his servants sought a young girl to 'lie in his bosom' and warm him back to life (I Kings i, 2).

DE PROFUNDIS CLAMAVI. 'Out of the depths have I cried . . .' Opening words of Psalm 130. It is always said or sung as part of the Catholic funeral service, and the words *De profundis* appear on many funeral notices, including Baudelaire's own.

DIVA, SUPPLICEM EXAUDI. 'Goddess, hear your votary's prayer.'

DU CAMP, MAXIME. Writer (1822–94). Friend of Flaubert, whom he accompanied on his journey to Egypt in 1849–50.

ÉLECTRE. Electra. In Greek legend and tragedy the daughter of Agamemnon and Clytemnestra, sister and faithful nurse to Orestes in his madness, wife to Pylades.

ÉPONINE. Eponina, Gaulish heroine, personification of virtue and marital devotion, was executed with her husband by the Romans in AD 78.

ÉRÈBE. Erebus, son of Chaos and Night, personified the darkness of the underworld. *L'Erèbe*, literary synonym for the underworld.

ESCHYLE. Aeschylus, ancient Greek tragedian.

EX-VOTO. Carving or small picture, usually in a precious material, hung before a shrine or image to commemorate a vow or show gratitude for prayers answered. The images of 41 imitate closely the iconography of the Virgin in Spanish painting.

F.N. Felix Nadar (1820–1910), caricaturist, pioneer photographer and balloonist.

FRASCATI. A gambling-house, restaurant and dancehall of this name was fashionable in Paris in the early years of the century; it closed in 1837.

GAVARNI. Lithographer and cartoonist (1804–66), he created and depicted fashionable female types. See Baudelaire's essay 'Quelques caricaturistes français'.

GUYS, CONSTANTIN. Artist and draughtsman (1805–92), he depicted fashionable Parisian life as well as reporting the Crimean War for the *Illustrated London News*. Baudelaire expressed great admiration for him in his long essay 'Le Peintre de la vie moderne'.

HARPAGON. Central character of Molière's *L'Avare* (*The Miser*).

HERCULE. Hercules, hero of Greek and Roman mythology, is said, as a baby, to have strangled two huge snakes which attacked him in his cradle.

HÉAUTONTIMOROUMÉNOS. 'The self-torturer' (Greek). Title of a comedy by Terence, Roman dramatist.

HERMÈS. 1. Hermes, the messenger of the gods in Greek myth.

2. Hermes Trismegistus, name given to the Egyptian god Thoth by Greek settlers, who ascribed to him the invention of alchemy.

HIPPOGRIFFE. Hippogriff, a mythical flying horse in medieval romances of chivalry and in Ariosto's *Orlando Furioso*.

ICARE. Icarus. In Greek legend he tried to fly with wings made of feathers and wax. The sun's rays melted the wax and he fell into the sea which was afterwards named after him.

ICARIE. Icaria, the island on which Icarus was buried.

J. G. F. It is not known to whom these initials refer, though Baudelaire also dedicated *Les Paradis artificiels* to her, saying that she had been another Electra (q.v.) to him in his sufferings.

LE JUIF ERRANT. The Wandering Jew. Christian legend tells how he refused to help Jesus on his way to crucifixion, and as a result was condemned to wander the earth, alone, for ever.

LAÏS. Lais, celebrated Greek courtesan (fifth century BC).

LAZARE. Lazarus, raised from the dead by Jesus Christ. When Jesus offers to raise Lazarus, his sister Martha objects, 'Lord, by this time he stinketh; for he hath been dead four days' (John xi, 39).

LÉTHÉ. Lethe, a river in the underworld. The dead drank its water to forget their past lives.

MÉGÈRE. Megaera, one of the three Furies of Greek myth. Hence French *une mégère*, a shrewish woman.

MICHEL-ANGE. Michelangelo Buonarroti (1475–1564), painter, sculptor and architect. His statue of *Night* is in the Medici Chapel, San Lorenzo, Florence.

MIDAS. Midas, a king in Greek legend who asked for and received the power of turning everything he touched into gold.

MINTURNES. Minturnae, Roman city surrounded by marshes.

MOESTA ET ERRABUNDA. 'Sad and wandering' (Latin).

MOÏSE. Moses. He struck the rock to produce water for the Israelites in the desert (Exodus xvii, 5–6).

OVIDE. Ovid, Roman poet (43 BC–AD 16). His *Tristia* are a lament for his exile from Rome. *'L'homme d'Ovide'* (53) refers to a passage in his *Metamorphoses* (ll. 84–5) where he says that man, unlike the other animals, has been given the privilege of holding his head high and is commanded to lift his face to the stars.

PHÉNIX. The Phoenix, in classical myth, was a fabulous bird which in old age burnt itself on a pyre and was reborn from its own ashes.

PHOEBÉ. Phoebe, the Moon (Greek).

PHOEBUS. Another name for Apollo, the god of music, poetry and light. In 3 it replaces (in 1861) *'le soleil'* (the sun).

PLUVIÔSE. One of the months (January–February) of the French revolutionary calendar, its name suggests 'rainy' (*pluvieux*), and here perhaps also Jupiter Pluvius, the Roman god of rain.

POMONE. Pomona, the Roman goddess of fruits and orchards. Statues of mythological subjects had been popular garden decorations from the sixteenth century onwards; in the nineteenth, plaster copies of the stone or terracotta originals were mass-produced to meet expanding demand.

PROSERPINE. Proserpina, Roman form of the Greek Persephone, virgin daughter of Demeter abducted to the underworld by Hades. She was allowed to return to earth each year for a period which coincided with the revival of vegetation in the spring.

PYLADE. Pylades, friend of Orestes in Greek legend; type of the faithful friend.

RENÉ. René is the hero of an extremely influential short fiction (1805) by Chateaubriand, who in his later *Mémoires d'outre-tombe* described his youthful passion for a Sylphide, a fairy-like being born of his own imagination.

ROQUEPLAN. Nestor Roqueplan, theatre director and drama critic (1804–70).

SAINTE-BEUVE. Charles-Augustin Sainte-Beuve (1804–69), poet, novelist and influential critic.

SALOMON. Solomon, Biblical King of Israel. An apocryphal work, the *Clavicules* ('Little Keys') was attributed to him. In 81 there is a pun on *clavicules*, meaning collar-bones.

SED NON SATIATA. 'But not satisfied'. The wording recalls Juvenal's description of the Empress Messalina coming home *'lassata viris, necdum satiata'* ('exhausted by men, but not yet satisfied' – *Satires* vi, 130).

SIMOÏS. Simois, a river near Troy. Virgil describes Andromache, exiled in Epirus, weeping for her husband on the banks of a river which recalled the Simois, *falsi Simoentis ad undam* (Aeneid III, 294–318). Baudelaire originally used this phrase as an epigraph to his poem.

SISYPHE. Sisyphus, whose punishment in the underworld was endlessly to roll a heavy stone uphill.

STERNE. Lawrence Sterne (1713–68), an English novelist much admired by French writers of Baudelaire's generation. The incident of the donkey and the macaroon appears in his *Tristram Shandy*.

STEVENS, JOSEPH. Belgian painter. His *Intérieur de saltimbanque* inspired poem 102, and he did give Baudelaire a fine waistcoat.

STYX. One of the rivers of the underworld; proverbially dark and gloomy.

SWEDENBORG. Emanuel Swedenborg (1688–1772). Swedish writer, exponent of unorthodox religious ideas, much read in France in the Romantic period.

TARTUFE. Tartuffe, hypocritical central character in Molière's play *Tartuffe*. Proverbial name for a hypocrite.

TE DEUM. A hymn of praise, beginning *Te Deum laudamus* ('We praise Thee, o God'), usually sung in ceremonies of celebration. In 5, *encenser* (to cense) also means to praise fulsomely, hence *jouer de l'encensoir*, to flatter unworthy objects.

THEOCRITUS. Greek poet (third century BC), writer of idylls and inventor of the pastoral mode.

THALIE. Thalia, Muse of comedy. Hence '*prêtresse de Thalie*', an actress (in pretentious journalistic language).

TIVOLI. 1. Tivoli, a small town near Rome, famous for the temples and villas which surround it.

2. In 55, a commercial pleasure-garden in Paris named after the town.

TORNÉO. A river in Sweden.

VÉNUSTRE. An illiterate pronunciation of *Vénus*.

VESTALE. A vestal virgin (Roman history). Proverbial for their chastity and retired life.

VEUILLOT. Louis Veuillot (1813–83), prolific Catholic journalist and polemicist, notorious for his use of slang and clichés. Surprisingly, a friend of Baudelaire.

INDEX OF TITLES AND
FIRST LINES